LET THEM ROT

 INVENTING WRITING THEORY

Jacques Lezra and Paul North, series editors

LET THEM ROT

ANTIGONE'S PARALLAX

ALENKA ZUPANČIČ

Fordham University Press   *New York 2023*

Library of Congress Cataloging-in-Publication Data available online at
https://catalog.loc.gov.

Printed in the United States of America

25 24 23   5 4 3 2 1

First edition

CONTENTS

PREFACE

It began with something rather accidental, though not without a basis in my earlier work on ethics, in which Antigone played some role. A dear friend and colleague, Dominiek Hoens, invited me to give a workshop on Antigone in Brussels in January 2020—that is to say, at the dawn of the first pandemic year. It was a one-afternoon event for which I prepared some notes and ideas to discuss with the participants. I would not call my talk there a work in progress, because at that time I didn't know or anticipate that there would be any "progress," anything further coming out of it. It was more like a construction site, with some (what I thought were) interesting ideas and a lot of loose ends. I really enjoyed and appreciated the discussion and sort of left Antigone there. And then, well into the first year of the pandemic and its lockdown, I returned to my notes, picking up a few loose ends, and started writing about Antigone again—with a surprising and unexpected ease and force driving my work. I do not want to say that the text "wrote itself," but the original "accident," the contingency that triggered my starting to think about Antigone, certainly began to look like a *necessity* and an enjoyable necessity at that. One thing led to another, as they say, and I followed the ideas as they kept coming, not knowing where it would all end up or if it would end up anywhere at all. An unexpected privilege of the standstill induced by the pandemic? Or perhaps the workings of a slightly peculiar state of mind, a mind closed in on itself, locked down upon itself?

Yet if this was madness, there was method in it. And it became clearer day by day, with regard to both general perspective and particular points of inquiry. There is probably no classical text that has inspired more interpretation, critical attention, and creative response than Sophocles's *Antigone*. The general perspective from which I read it could be summarized with this simple question: What is it about the figure of Antigone that keeps haunting us? Why do all these readings and rewritings keep emerging? To what kind of (always) contemporary contradiction does the need, the urge to reread and reimagine *Antigone*—in all kinds of contexts and languages—correspond?

As key anchor points of this general interrogation, three particular "obsessions" have driven my writing and thinking about *Antigone*. First, her violence. And I do not use this term simply pejoratively, as it is most often used today. Nor do I mean the graphic violence to which we have become so accustomed in movies and in the media. By and large, the violence in *Antigone* is the opposite of "graphic"; it is sharp and piercing. It takes up almost no space but goes straight to the bone. It is the violence of words, the violence of principles, the violence of desire, the violence of subjectivity. It is a violence quite different from the one that Creon wields; it is a violence that does not come from Power and what it can do but nevertheless amounts to a considerable power. What is this violence? How to conceive of it, both philosophically and politically? Although chapter 1 focuses explicitly on these questions, they run throughout the text.

Then there is the issue of funerary rites and their role in appeasing the specific "undeadness" that seems to be the other side of human life, its irreducible undercurrent that death alone cannot end and put to rest. This issue prompted an investigation into the relationship between language, sexuality (sexual reproduction), death, "second death," and a peculiar nonlinguistic Real that occurs as a by-product of language yet is not reducible (back) to language or to the symbolic.

And then there is what probably "obsessed" me the most in my writing, namely, Antigone's statement that if it were her children or husband lying unburied out there, she would let them rot (*tékō*) and not take it upon herself to defy the decree of the state. How does this exclusivist, singularizing claim (she would do it only for Polyneices), which she uses to describe the "unwritten law" she follows, accord with Antigone's universal appeal and compelling power? The attempt to answer this question led, step by step, to the interrogation of what this particular (Oedipal) family's misfortune (*átē*), of which Antigone chooses to be the guardian, shares with the general condition of humanity? It led to the question, "What is incest?"; to the hypothesis of a certain "incestuous" dimension of language; and to the possibility of universal relevance of a violent subjective desire.

Clearly, these are by no means minor preoccupations or "obsessions," and there is certainly enough in them to drive one's thinking and writing fervently for a while. At the same time, I really wanted to stick to these—and only these—Ariadne threads while I was finding my way around the constellation called Antigone. The argument follows, I hope, a fairly rigorous logic or necessity. And the inherent logic that directed my questioning has also led me to take certain turns rather than others and follow their course. Among the many seminal contributions to the Antigone debate, I have chosen to include only the contributions with which I was working in developing my points and hence to cite only those authors who have a direct place in the construction of my argument. *Let Them Rot: Antigone's Parallax* is not intended to be a polemical text, although its arguments clearly differ from those of some other readings. It is more like a specific philosophical "intervention" in a broad and prominent field of study. The ambition of this book is thus both very modest and very immodest. It is modest because it really wants to intervene only at some precise points of what takes place in Sophocles's *Antigone*. It is not so modest because it assumes, at least implicitly, that these specific or localized points have effects and consequences that affect the constellation of *Antigone* in its entirety—and perhaps extend beyond it.

The result of my "obsessions" regarding Antigone is perhaps somewhat unorthodox as far as Antigone scholarship goes. Or maybe it is not. In any case, I would like to thank Paul North, Thomas Lay, and Jacques Lezra for recognizing the merits of this text and deeming it just right for their Idiom series. Their active—I am tempted to say "militant," if that word were not tainted with a suspicious undertone—support has made this publication possible.

LET THEM ROT

PROLOGUE: "A HOT MIND OVER CHILLY THINGS"

Sophocles wrote *Antigone* in or before 441 BCE, in a world that was in many ways almost unimaginably different from our own. And yet the figure of Antigone continues to haunt our imaginations and influence our thinking about a whole range of different ideas and battles, including very modern ones. Over forty different adaptations of *Antigone* have appeared in the past hundred years, not to mention many "creative" translations and countless readings—philosophical and otherwise—of the play. If we take just the past six years, several new adaptations have appeared. Two of them, both from 2017 (Stefan Hertmans's poetic monologue *Antigone in Molenbeek* and Kamila Shamsie's novel *Home Fire*), place Antigone in the context of terrorism and the contemporary "war on terror"; one (Sophie Deraspe's film *Antigone* [2019]) places her in the context of the recent refugee crisis; while Slavoj Žižek's *Antigone* (2016) rewrites the play with three alternative endings and invents a powerful way of introducing a third element—the chorus as collective subject—into the usual and well-rehearsed theme of the relationship between the individual and the state.

It is certainly not unusual for a classical play or hero to receive many different versions and readings ("interpretations"), but *Antigone* is still quite exceptional. Antigone is also exceptional for the many really interesting versions of herself she has instigated—instigated rather than inspired, because fire seems to be much more associated with the effect Antigone produces with her "cold," inflexible persistence. "You have a hot mind over chilly things," Ismene says to her in the dialog that opens the play. This expression is indeed quite inspired, and it goes against the common mantra and prescription according to which we need a cold mind to deal with heated things: the worst things and situations are chilly, rather that hot, and it takes a very hot mind to truly engage with them and make others do as well.

The fact that there are so many strong versions of the play points to something very ingenious in the way the original drama is constructed. For although we talk about different versions (implying difference, differentiation), all the really good ones also reproduce something: they manage to repeat, or perhaps re-create, reactivate, some singularity of the constellation called "Antigone," as laid out in the original play.

Generally speaking, it seems that Antigone comes into focus (of rewriting and interpretation) every time there is some significant tectonic shift or crisis in the social fabric, in the symbolic structuring of the law, or in the wider realm of morality or *Sittlichkeit*. More specifically, perhaps, the figure of Antigone seems to be emblematic of a particular kind of social antagonism that touches on the question of the very constitution, and being, of the social. Thus, if we wish to pin down the "eternally" present, relevant singularity of the play, antagonism might be the first step in defining it. But antagonism should in this case be understood not as hostility and conflict between two (or several) elements but rather in the sense in which Marx talked about "class antagonism": not simply as conflict *between* different classes and their interests but as something that pertains to the very logic of the space, or reality, in which these classes exist—in this case, the reality of the capitalist mode of production. In other words, talking about antagonism in the case of Antigone is meant to direct our attention not to her conflict with and opposition to Creon but rather to something that surfaces *in* and *through* this conflict, something that brings to the fore a singular torsion, or crack, which defines the very ground they stand on in their conflict. This is the double perspective and hence the power of Antigone as a figure who not only stands her ground in her opposition to Creon but makes us perceive the otherwise invisible constitutive elements, exceptions, and dialectical tensions of the social space. What we are presented with is thus not simply a conflict between the two protagonists as two elements of reality but an impossible glimpse of what constitutes this reality and belies its status as a neutral medium in which different positions appear and enter into conflict. This is why the singular way in which we as readers or viewers of *Antigone* experience the play would perhaps be best described by the term "parallax view": a simultaneous existence of two perspectives that normally never meet or exist on the same plane. And yet here, in Sophocles's play, that is exactly what happens: they meet.

Antigone is not such a great text because the play "gives us much to think about" or "presents us with a difficult (moral) dilemma." If we go down the road of questioning whether Antigone is right or not to demand what she demands and focusing on that to the exclusion of everything else, I think we miss the whole point and power of the play. She *is* what she does and demands, and her actions reveal, expose, something in the order and structure of which she is a part, much more than they reveal something about herself. Her act—covering Polyneices's body—and her demand constitute the *inaugural* fact (or should we say event?) of the play; although Antigone certainly has reasons for her actions, and enumerates some of them, her act nevertheless appears to be the absolute starting point, which then has consequences for both past and future. In this respect, Antigone is like Hamlet without the figure of the ghost appearing as a distinct character. To put it more precisely, if in *Hamlet* everything begins with the apparition of the ghost and his words, then in *Antigone* there is not even a ghost of authority testifying to the wrong that took place; it is all about Antigone's subjective and subjectivizing conviction (her "hot mind"); this is why we could say that it is her own appearance and actions that have a ghostly aftereffect, create a spectral but irreducible afterimage that persists throughout the play. We could also say that rather than "presenting us with a difficult (moral) dilemma" and "giving us a lot to think about," *the play drops something on us*, discharges something on us that is what it is, even if we don't fully understand what it is. It works on us. It works through us. It gives us something; it transmits something "impossible" and unfamiliar. The headache it can give us is caused not by overthinking this or that dilemma but by something more like a *glitch* or almost a visual challenge of seeing, in one and the same frame, both the reality and its constitutive inherent twist—hence the idea of parallax view.

It is thus important to emphasize that the two levels or points of view at issue in this parallax are not simply those of Antigone and Creon, though their confrontation certainly helps to bring to light the parallax gap we are trying to define. Nor is this simply a matter of confrontation between state power or state laws and some other, eternal, unwritten ethical or divine laws. Here, it is indeed very important to determine what exactly is the status of the divine, unwritten laws that Antigone famously invokes at one point and that she believes Creon is violating. But before we address this question, two further opening remarks seem necessary.

First, the story of Antigone implies and presupposes the other two stories of the so-called Theban Trilogy, *Oedipus the King* and *Oedipus at Colonus*. Key elements of these two plays are at the heart of the tragedy of *Antigone* and cannot be separated from it. The fact that Sophocles, although the order of the plays narratively is *Oedipus the King*, *Oedipus at Colonus*, and then *Antigone*, wrote *Antigone* first, clearly indicates that the other two plays, or their basic narrative elements, were present from the beginning as inherent elements of the constellation called "Antigone." It also illustrates my point about Antigone's actions being an absolute beginning: something that implies (its own) history rather than follows from it.

My second remark, related to the first, is that Creon is not simply a ruler, a king, a figure of state power, under whose rule the events described take place. He comes to power only when the two brothers (Polyneices and Eteocles, both sons of Oedipus) kill each other. The edict that honors one brother and excludes the other from burial rites is not simply one of his edicts but is his inaugural act, the act in this case coinciding with the constitution of power. This is by no means insignificant, and it is pregnant with implications. Moreover, we are not dealing merely with a change of power, a change of ruler, the replacement of one king by another, but—in the wider Sophoclean perspective—a change from, say, the blameless but no less unspeakably "criminal" rule associated with Oedipus (who, unbeknown to himself, has killed King Laius, his own father, taken his place, and married his mother, Jocasta) to a "civilized," normal, business-as-usual rule. This tectonic shift is at the very heart of Sophocles's play.

Let us briefly recall the background story. Polyneices and Eteocles, the two sons from the incestuous relationship, were to share the kingdom after the exile of Oedipus, each taking a one-year reign in turn. However, Eteocles refused to cede his throne after his year as king. Therefore, Polyneices raised an army to oust Eteocles from his throne, and a battle ensued. At the end of the battle, the brothers killed each other, after which Jocasta's brother, Creon, ascended the throne.[1] He decided that Polyneices was the traitor and therefore should not be accorded funeral rites. (In Jean Anouilh's version of *Antigone*, Creon cynically refers to this decision as a necessary

---

1. This part of the story also provides the starting point of Aeschylus's tragedy *Seven Against Thebes*, as well as Euripides's *The Suppliants* and *The Phoenician Women*. There is no doubt that Eteocles breaks the original agreement and usurps the crown, provoking Polyneices's attack. Based on these other plays, there is also no doubt that Creon's punishment of Polyneices—leaving his body exposed—is based neither on human nor divine law and is in fact an excess.

constitutive myth he had to offer his people, choosing quite arbitrarily one brother as the traitor and the other as the hero; he tells Antigone that it is not even clear whose disfigured remains belonged to which brother, so it could also be Eteocles's remains that lie unburied out there. This explicit addition is, of course, very modern: the addition of a reflexive surplus knowledge, a cynical recognition of the bad or dirty things that "we," the rulers, must do as a necessary part of the job, the recognition of the necessity and constitutive dirtiness of all political leadership—as if this explicit recognition made it less problematic and morally better. I will return later to the way this logic is often played out in the contemporary social and political context.)

To repeat, the major shift in the background of *Antigone* is the shift from the rule of Oedipus and his descendants, with the terrible curse and the unconscious crime shaping their destiny, to the "normal" rule of Creon; we could also say that what is at stake here, at least in some respects, is the transition from prehistory (myth) to history, from the rule of an unconscious crime pertaining to the law to the "rule of law" and *its* excluded, unconscious core. But in this concrete case the transition at stake is marked by Creon's inaugural excess and hubris, which stains the "normal rule" with an ineffaceable pathology, or pulls this pathology into the very core of the "normal rule". We could also use here an image to which I will have frequent recourse in the pages that follow—this transition is very much like the passage or shift at issue in the following joke: "We're not cannibals; we ate the last one yesterday."

What happens in *Antigone*, then, has to do with something implicit in the *constitution* of the normal social order. It has to do with a very specific, singular moment, with a forced normalization and generalization of that moment, and with its consequences for state power in its everyday, normal course or functioning. There is something in Creon's treatment of state power that violates the respect for the gap of the unconscious that pertains to the law, and it is here that we will locate the central point of violence as perceived by

Antigone, one with which Antigone's own violence is also intimately connected.

In what follows, I propose to work through some of the sensitive points with which Antigone confronts us (*durcharbeiten*, "working through"—a famous, and very suggestive, Freudian term): sensitive, virulent, contagious, powerful, disturbing, but also fascinating, with all the ambiguity of that term. Fascinating images attract, capture our gaze, but also blind us, prevent us from seeing. One of the many powerful observations Lacan makes in his commentary on *Antigone* concerns precisely the heroine's status as a central image. When we see the play performed onstage, he suggests, we are spectators only in relation to Antigone—in relation to the rest of the play, we are more like "listeners." Only Antigone necessarily emerges as an image, with a blinding splendor, with a "sublime beauty" that, of course, has nothing to do with her physical appearance.

There are several such sensitive points in connection with Antigone. I will highlight and discuss three, which could be roughly placed under the following strongly interrelated headings: violence and unwritten laws; death and funeral rites; incest and desire— or, from another, parallax perspective: terror, undeadness, and sublimation.

1

VIOLENCE, TERROR, AND UNWRITTEN LAWS

Could we say that the play begins with Antigone committing an act of "subjective violence" when she covers Polyneices's corpse, thus violating the laws (decrees) of the state ruled by Creon, who embodies "objective" or "systemic" violence? The difference, then, would imply the difference between a *visibly* violent interruption (by Antigone) of the more or less smooth flow of things and the *invisible* violence involved in maintaining that very smooth flow of things (and embodied in Creon's decrees).[1]

I believe the answer is no, not really, because the core of Antigone's rebellion lies in her assertion that something related to state

1. In general terms, this difference is most concisely explained by Slavoj Žižek: "The catch is that subjective and objective violence cannot be perceived from the same standpoint: subjective violence is experienced as such against the background of a non-violent zero level. It is seen as perturbation of the 'normal,' peaceful state of things. However, objective violence is precisely the violence inherent to this 'normal' state of things. Objective violence is invisible since it sustains the very zero-level standard against which we perceive something subjectively violent. . . . It may be invisible, but it has to be taken into account if one is to make sense of what otherwise seem to be 'irrational' explosions of subjective violence" (2008, 2).

laws has been violated by Creon himself. By forbidding Polyneices's burial, Creon has not simply perpetuated the standard, imperceptible objective/systemic violence of the given rule but has himself performed a gesture of excessive, subjective violence. Moreover—and this aggravates his offense—he has performed this gesture of subjective violence *in the name of the state* and public law.

By forbidding the burial of Polyneices, Creon transgresses his public, state office. But why? This is a very important question, on which much depends.

A conventional answer we often get, for example, is that the issue here is the separation, the divide, between the private and the public, and that by forbidding the burial, Creon is intruding into the realm of another law—private or familial—that Antigone chooses to defend, as if we were dealing with two juxtaposed laws that refer to different domains. Antigone does indeed invoke unwritten laws, but it is by no means clear what they are and—as we shall see, and as many critics have already noted—even less clear in what way they would command her to do what she does.[2] With regard to the opposition private/public, the whole play shows that in the case of Antigone, this division is not really operative. Antigone embodies, as it were, the very *untenability* of this separation. It is extremely problematic to present Antigone as the guardian of family values or as the keeper of the "home fires" in the sense of a safe haven or a refuge that offers us protection from external misfortune or simply from public affairs. As Shamsie captures perfectly with the title of her novel, "home fire" in Antigone's case chimes directly with conflagration and with the *political/public* implications of her actions (rather than with any kind of domestic sentiment). We could even argue that Antigone is an emblematic ancient embodiment of the contemporary slogan "the private is the political."

My first suggestion would be that what Creon violates is not some other law (unwritten, divine laws) but an unwritten dimension of his

2. Particularly if we bear in mind her explicit statement that she wouldn't do it if anybody else were at stake—she wouldn't do it for her children or for her husband. I'll discuss this aspect of her claim in chapter 3.

own law. It is not simply some other laws that are at stake or the outer limits of public laws, limits that would restrict the scope of those laws (and suggest, for example, that they have no authority over the dead and over death); rather, it is a matter of the other side of public, written laws. Let me try to explain and develop this idea by using the cannibal joke evoked earlier: "We're not cannibals; we ate the last one yesterday."

What this joke nicely sums up is that at the core of every written, symbolic law there is (always) something like an "impossible crime." If a civilized, noncannibal community is constituted by its members eating the last cannibal, that community could never be constituted if that "last" act of cannibalism were labeled as such, a criminal act of cannibalism. From the standpoint of the new community, it is a crime but only retrospectively; it is a crime that becomes a crime with the very occurrence of this act of eating the "last." It is not a crime like other crimes; it is, strictly speaking, the impossible crime that takes place in a territory that has no territory, no ground on which to stand; it constitutes an excluded interior of the state of law. The constitution of law (or of the symbolic order in general) involves a *discontinuity*, a gap, something that cannot be based on anything other than itself or derived linearly from the previous, "natural state." The cannibal joke points to just that. "Eating the last cannibal" would correspond to the linear transition from one state to another, without discontinuity, but this is logically impossible; it constitutes a paradox: What about those who ate the last cannibal? In what way are they no longer cannibals? Something happens here; something is lost, the first, "original generation" of noncannibals is constitutively missing, and the law of noncannibalism depends on its absence, on this gap. One could argue that this kind of gap is inherent in all symbolic laws.

So this paradoxical crime has no symbolic status; it exists as a gap. And this gap is considered a sacred realm, a realm of the divine, of unwritten laws, of taboos.[3] Symbolic (public, state) law or rule

---

3. I am not arguing that this is the only possible definition of the sacred or the only mode in which it exists, but it certainly is an important one and one that plays a key role in *Antigone*.

begins with and depends on a crime that has never been prosecuted as such. This crime is transfigured into the realm of the sacred—the impossible territory implicit in the very operation of public laws, the realm that we are to keep out and respect by precisely not going there and not turning it into yet another territory of business-as-usual. If this respect is about protecting the crime that is at stake in the constitution of state laws, it is in a very precise sense of the term "protect." The protecting at issue here is not simply about keeping it hidden, keeping it a dirty secret; rather, it is about keeping this criminal core from being drawn into the everyday workings of the rule of law and thus from turning into the dirty but powerful secret weapon—supposedly "necessary"—of this or that empirical rule.

If we take all this seriously, it has an important consequence. From this perspective, the "sacred," unwritten laws evoked by Antigone are not simply a remnant of ancient traditions but arise (or appear) with the cut that inaugurates the new order—it is only at this point that a particular dimension of the old past is constituted as sacred because it is linked to the inaugurating crime of the new order. The sacred could thus be defined in this context as something that has no place in the given symbolic order; more precisely, the place of the sacred is the place of the nonplace. It is precisely at this point, and in precisely this sense, that the "sacred" forms the inner limit of symbolic, public law. The inner limit of symbolic law means that the law does not hold at some point of its own edifice, that its barrier (the barrier that the law erects) is porous: that *there is a hole in the fence*, to use a suggestive image. That hole in the fence is the last cannibal we ate; and there is nothing in the law that can directly patch that hole, the leak it implies. So I would argue that here, at this point, a considerable number of what are called unwritten laws come into play. It is the unwritten laws—laws that exist not in an explicit symbolic form but as something we simply and "naturally" live by—that protect, surround, make us respect (keep our distance from) the impossible point of the constitution of the symbolic (public) laws and say something like, *Don't go too close to the leak, to the hole. Respect it! Keep your distance!* In this perspective, the written, public laws and the unwritten laws are not simply two realms or domains but are intimately (or "extimately") connected by and *in* this impossible point: unwritten laws are there to protect and regulate access to the leak/hole at the heart of public law. They are not in direct opposition to it.

The refusal of a burial is a blatant case of playing with this limit of the law: it is indeed, and quite literally, *pushing the limit* of the symbolic law—it is pushing it at the precise point where it is porous; it is playing with fire. We might put it yet another way: it means that Creon is using his symbolic power (as ruler of the state) to deny the impossibility inherent in its constitution and to usurp it instead as a direct source of his power. He uses it to demonstrate and consolidate his power after the fight between two brothers and crown pretenders, who—rather conveniently for Creon—killed each other. Creon eats the last cannibal in public. Or, perhaps more accurately, Creon stages the feast of eating the last cannibal and invites everyone to see his decaying body. Another significant word that comes to mind in this connection is "decency," with "obscenity" as its opposite. The image of the obscene feast that Creon creates with his decisions is quite explicit in the text; it is particularly prominent in the final dialog between Teiresias and Creon, the dialog that finally makes Creon change his mind and reverse his decision—only it is too late, Antigone has already hanged herself in her tomb. This is the picture Teiresias paints for Creon:

> All of the altars of the town are choked
> with leavings of the dogs and birds; their feast
> was on that fated, fallen son of Oedipus.
> So the gods accept no offering from us,
> not prayer, nor flame of sacrifice. The birds
> cry out a sound that I cannot distinguish,
> gorged with the greasy blood of that dead man.
> . . . .
> Yield to the dead. Why goad him where he lies?
> What use to kill the dead a second time? (*Antigone*, 1017–1030)[4]

4. Unless otherwise indicated, all translations of the plays are from Sophocles 2013.

"Obscenity" describes Creon's actions and their consequences quite well. And we could say that the important dividing line that applies in relation to the unwritten laws is precisely that between decency and obscenity. As I have already indicated, the unwritten laws do not refer to something else, as the public laws do; they refer to a certain (or perhaps we should say uncertain) *dimension* of the public laws. To respect this unwritten dimension is to show a certain decency; to violate it is tantamount to obscenity. Any empirical content that appears at this point can only be obscene.

Let us say, then, that it is Creon who is the first to violate something, to push the limit of the symbolic law (*What use to kill the dead a second time?*). And he does so by using this very law, by invoking it. Antigone is challenged by this; she responds to it, reacts violently to it—not on some abstract-general level, of course. She does it and claims that she does it only because her brother is at stake. There is an absolute singularity attached to her principle, and I will return to the meaning of that singularity in chapter 3. Creon then pushes the limit even further—and this constitutes both the center and the central image of the play—by condemning *her* to be buried alive. This, then, is Creon's double violation as described by Teiresias in the same dialog:

> You settled a living person without honor
> in a tomb; you keep up here that which belongs
> below, a corpse unburied and unholy.
> Not you, nor any god of high should have
> any business with this. The violation's yours. (*Antigone*, 1069–1073)

Or, in another, freer, yet more suggestive translation (by the same translator):

> You sent a life to settle in a tomb;
> You keep up here that which belongs below
> The corpse unburied, robbed of its release. (*Antigone*, 1069–1071)

These two acts of Creon do not play simply with life and death but with something beyond life and death: they aim, as it were, at a third something. Antigone is not simply condemned to death, punished by death for her actions. She is punished by this additional twist: that she is forced to *live her death*, that she is buried alive. This is a very harsh punishment and a way of explicitly introducing the dimension "between two deaths," as Lacan has called it (Lacan 1997, 270). Not only Polyneices but Antigone also will not get a proper burial; she will be walled up alive in a tomb. This even becomes the central image of the play: this impossible place, this nonplace between two deaths. And it definitely tells us something about Creon—he seems obsessed, fascinated by this limit of the law and by pushing it. This appears to be his *hamartia*, his fatal flaw. And, not surprisingly, Creon himself ends up in the same place. After all of his loved ones have committed suicide as a result of what he set in motion with his decree, the messenger describes him with these words: "Call him a breathing corpse" (*Antigone*, 1167).

So Antigone responds to Creon's decree; she acts. She does not respond by organizing a civil movement to protect basic human rights—no more so in contemporary versions than she does in Sophocles's original. There is something wrong with readings of Antigone that portray her as the guardian and protector of an essential and universal humanity. This is not about "everyone, even the worst criminal, has a right to a burial." It is about something much more specific, though—as I will try to show later—of no less universal bearing. For now, let us simply say that Antigone makes a claim, raises the stakes, and persists there, beyond the limit and the question of good and beyond the end—rather than to the end. More specifically, her attitude is one of *perseverance*, which is different from the *fixation* that characterizes Creon. Joan Copjec has argued this important point compellingly.[5]

---

5. In *Three Essays on the Theory of Sexuality*, Freud warns us not to conflate *Fixiertheit*, which is an inexplicable fixation that persists despite every external attempt to dislodge it, with *Haftbarkeit*, "which is perhaps best translated by 'perseverance' but has a curious resonance in German, since it also means 'responsibility,' 'commitment.'" It is this distinction

Antigone responds to Creon's pushing the limit by establishing her own way of pushing the limit or of making Creon push the limit all the way through, until the symbolic law, the limit of which he pushes, crashes on him and the rest of the city. Obviously, this is not simply a personal matter, yet the public law and its (in)justice here touch on something very personal—or should I say, rather, something very singular? Yet this personal singularity is itself at the core of public law (of Thebes)—this, I believe, is Antigone's fundamental assertion: that in this case the personal is *directly* political, that it very much concerns the public sphere, so to speak.

In making and insisting on her particular claim,[6] Antigone aims not so much at an all-encompassing universality ("we are all human beings") as at a principle. Her justice is principled, saying something like, *You cannot push this limit, play with it, without consequences.* To argue and prove her point (and her justice), *she is willing to be that consequence*; she feels she can't help but be that consequence. Here lies her ethical stake and her difference from (at play in her indifference toward) her sister, Ismene. Ismene claims that as women they are powerless to do anything about the situation, that all action is useless, pointless.[7] But Antigone knows this; she knows that her actions will not make Creon change his mind and bury Polyneices. But it would be wrong to say that she persists just for the sake of persisting; she persists because she knows that she can embody the consequences of Creon's ruling and the violence of his decree for all

---

introduced by Freud that lies behind and undergirds Lacan's insistence that Antigone, and she alone, is the heroine of Sophocles' play; her *perseverance* in carrying out the burial of her brother is ethically different from Creon's *fixation* on enforcing the statist prohibition against the burial (Copjec 2002, 16).

6. It was of course Judith Butler who elevated the term "Antigone's claim" to the conceptual level with the title of her book on Antigone (Butler 2000).

7.

We must remember that we two are women,
so not to fight with men;
and that since we are subject to stronger power
we must hear these orders, or any that may be worse. (*Antigone*, 61–64)

to see. This is something that is within *her* power, even if she is only
"a woman."

Why is this stake ethical? Because the fact that you can't play with
that limit without consequences applies in practice only when you
have someone like Antigone as your antagonist: someone who is willing to be that consequence. There is no objective necessity in this
consequence. Antigone is the antagonist par excellence. By this I
mean that rulers and leaders do not usually have antagonists like that,
and for this reason they tend to get away with crossing the line. Their
power protects them, intimidates potential antagonists, crashes
(onto) them.

This kind of pushing the limit of symbolic law could be seen
as the point we, in the modern context, usually associate with
state violence—which is not the same thing as systemic violence: it is
about the often illegal practices to which state power can resort simply because it is the state, for example, things like "enhanced interrogation techniques" invoked in the novel *Home Fire*. Perfectly legal,
respectable states (not just "rogue states") carry out all sorts of illegal
practices, sometimes outsourcing them and making sure they don't
happen on their territory. This includes dirty work done by all sorts
of intelligence agencies and the military as part of clandestine or not-
so-clandestine operations. It is very difficult to challenge the state
when it does this—take Julian Assange, another Antigone-like figure
of our time. He insisted that a massive state wrong be exposed and
was almost literally buried alive as punishment.

Modern illegal state violence (or, more generally, illegal or extralegal practices supported and enabled by the legally existing appa-
ratuses of power) could be seen as a contemporary version of
Creon's way of ruling *shamelessly*, that is to say, by transgressing
the inner limits of the law, by repeating its illegal constitution—
like eating the last cannibal *over and over again*. We could also
describe this configuration in these terms: instead of experiencing
the original, constitutive crime of the law as the "impossible" from
which one must keep away, this crime becomes a *special weapon* that

one constantly has at one's disposal, that one uses more or less secretly, that one reactivates in all kinds of empirical, present situations. And we should add that in our times this is not even done very secretly. There seems to be a new species of leaders emerging who take pride in committing this crime openly rather than secretly, as if it amounted to some kind of fundamental moral difference or difference of character, namely, "having the courage," "the guts," to do it openly. But what may appear to be their courageous transgression of state laws by avoiding the "hypocrisy" that those laws sometimes demand is nothing more than a direct identification with the obscene other side of state power itself. It does not amount to anything else or different. They are "transgressing" their own laws. This is why, even when they are in power, these leaders continue to act as if they are in opposition to the existing power, rebelling against it—call it the "deep state" or something else. Certainly these leaders still do many things in secret, but bragging about transgressions and impunity for them has become their major selling point. Remember, for example, Donald Trump's boast, "I could stand in the middle of Fifth Avenue and shoot someone, and I wouldn't lose any voters."[8] Unlike classical state power (which has never really been "sexy"), this defines the libidinal appeal of the new populisms and their leaders. It seems indeed that our current historical moment is defined primarily by the bleak alternative and oscillation between "bureaucracy" and "transgression," between secret and open, obscene state power.

In connection with this impunity of power, a brief remark on terrorism seems appropriate. In the modern context, Antigone in particular is often associated with terrorism, or some dimension of terror, and not without reason. As recent examples we have Shamsie's[9]

8. https://www.theguardian.com/us-news/2016/jan/24/donald-trump-says-he-could-shoot-somebody-and-still-not-lose-voters.

9. Her novel *Home Fire* (2017) sets the story of Antigone in the context of British Muslims. The novel follows the Pasha family: twin siblings Aneeka and Parvaiz and their older sister,

and Hertmans's[10] versions of the play, but this parallel was in fact drawn some time ago, with Volker Schlöndorff's "Antigone," which was part of the famous omnibus *Germany in Autumn* (1978). The film was banned because of its striking parallel to the situation in Germany when members of the terrorist group Rote Armee Fraktion (RAF) died mysteriously in prison and were denied a public funeral. Antigone thus resonated strongly in this "terrorist context." In some ways, at least, the logic underlying the actions of the RAF or the Red Brigades was that of combating state violence by emulating it. The basic argument went something like this: What you, state powers, call "terrorism" is simply state violence without a state, without a state *covering up* or supporting this (illegal) violence. The state as such relies on terror, involves terror as its obscene other side.

It is also important to emphasize in this context that Antigone seems to occupy two positions simultaneously in the configuration of terror: she wants to bury the terrorists (those who are declared terrorists by the state), thus symbolically acknowledging their existence and death; but her act of perseverance and persistence is in itself perceived as an act of terror, a terrorist act by which she also becomes the enemy of the state; she is seen as even more "terrorist"

Isma, who has raised them in the years since the death of their mother; their jihadi father, whom the twins never knew, is also dead. Parvaiz attempts to follow in his father's footsteps by joining ISIS in Syria. He soon decides he has made a serious mistake and his twin sister attempts to help him return to Britain, in part through her romantic relationship with Eamonn Lone, son of British Home Secretary Karamat Lone, who has built his political career on his rejection of his own Muslim background. The effort to bring Parvaiz home fails when he is shot to death trying to escape ISIS, then Eamonn and Aneeka, trying to return Parvaiz's body to the UK over the objections of Karamat Lone, die in a terrorist attack.

10. With his "poetic monologue," *Antigone in Molenbeek*, Stefan Hertmans has adapted Sophocles' tragedy to our contemporary, multicultural society. Antigone is now known as Nouria, a brave young law student from the Brussels district of Molenbeek. Just as in the classic, she wants to pay her last respects to her deceased brother—in Hertmans's version a suicide bomber—and bury his remains. But the authorities decide otherwise. Here the lawmaker is not a perfidious state, but district police officer Crénom, a representative of our fearful democratic society.

than the original terrorists themselves.[11] The template of this argument is this: Even if she is *right* in her claim that what happened was highly problematic, her insistence and persistence in that claim are *wrong* (they are even more dangerous than what the state did). We have seen this argument openly repeated in the case of Assange, as well as in those of several whistleblowers: they were presented as the real terrorists or true enemies (of the state). The ease with which the term "terrorist" is used today to dismiss those critics who point to the obscene, "terrorist" other side of state power could be seen as a clear indication of the growing reliance of state power itself on that other, obscene side. It would also be possible to see it as a symptom of the disintegration of the state in many of its aspects, particularly those where it is supposed to provide the infrastructure of the commons and of public interest.

The question of the state as a possible symbolic cover-up of excessive, extralegal violence is also at stake in the question of funerary rites and their violation. But why, exactly? we might ask. What is it about the denial of funerary rites that seems to go right to the heart of the problem of excessive use of symbolic power, which in turn undermines symbolic power itself?

We are obviously not done with the question of violence, but it is time to bring in another vital point or subpoint of *Antigone* that is related to the question of violence: burial rites and their violation.

---

11. Or, as Lacan would put it, Antigone "is there in spite of herself as victim and holocaust" (1997, 282).

DEATH, UNDEADNESS, AND FUNERAL RITES

Despite its deserved fame in this context, Sophocles's *Antigone* is not, of course, the only ancient Greek text to focus on the question of burying the dead. Rather, in *Antigone* Sophocles takes up a motif whose sensitivity and topicality were not only deeply woven into Greek culture but also constituted an important part of its internal dynamics and formed the source of many stories and pre-stories. The struggle over the bodies of the deceased and their burial is one of the key threads of the *Iliad*, the bodies of Patroclus and Hector being most representative of this. Leaving the corpses unburied, exposing them to vultures, and actively mistreating them (e.g., having them dragged by horses through dust, mud, and rocks) was all part of a "special warfare" aimed at killing the heroes a second time, and was considered even more unbearable for their family and friends than their death itself. This was not an uncommon practice (especially in wartime), and yet was persistently perceived as excessive and, yes, disapproved of by the gods. The starting point and basis for the story of Euripides's *The Suppliants* is directly related to the (pre-)story of Antigone. The mothers of the slayed heroes who fought together

21

with Polyneices to help him return to Thebes after he had been ousted by Eteocles's usurpation of power—the part of the story that is the subject of Aeschylus's *Seven Against Thebes* and Euripides's *The Phoenician Women*—come together to plead for the release of the corpses. Creon thus also prevented the burial of the other heroes who fought and were killed at the gates of Thebes, and the return (and burial) of their corpses is the central theme of *The Suppliants*. A few fragments from Euripides's play will suffice to illustrate the high sensitivity of this theme.

> So now their mothers would bury in the grave the dead,
> whom the spear has slain, but the victors prevent them
> and will not allow them to take up the corpses,
> holding the laws of the gods in no honor. (*The Suppliants*, 16–19)[1]

> At your knees I fall, aged lady,
> and my old lips beseech you;
> the lawless ones
> —rescue my children!—
> those who left the limbs of the dead,
> relaxed in death, a prey to mountain beasts; (*The Suppliants*, 42–47)

> and persuade your son, O, we implore you,
> to go unto the river Ismenus,
> and place within my arms the bodies of the dead,
> slain in their prime and wandering without a tomb.
>   (*The Suppliants*, 59–62)

From this broader mythological, historical, and political context, it is clear, first, that Antigone is not demanding anything special or unusual, but something that is considered part of normal mores and decency, which also the worldly powers must respect and follow. Creon systematically violates this. The confrontation between Theseus and the Theban Herald sent by Creon is clearly about a clash

---

1. This and the subsequent quotes refer to *The Suppliants* published in Perseus Digital Library: http://www.perseus.tufts.edu/hopper/text?doc=Perseus:text:1999.01.0122.

between two kinds of (worldly) rule: a "despotic" one (Creon is called a "despot," a "tyrant" who rules arbitrarily and solely for his own benefit), and a "democratic" one.[2]

In this Greek context, then, it is quite clear that the origin of the problem lies with Creon rather than with Antigone, and that their confrontation is not about the difference between the state (and public laws) and the private realm (i.e., family traditions and laws). Creon does not simply embody the state, but a very particular state and a very *personal* form of rule and state. Although there is no doubt that Antigone also has something "particular" about her, and that her way of acting and justifying these actions is by no means simply reducible to the figure of a fighter for universal human rights (we will discuss this "particularity" in more detail in the next chapter). Yet, to repeat: her effort to bury Polyneices is something quite "natural," ordinary. What is not ordinary and indeed breaks with custom is the fact that she, as a woman, takes it upon herself to act, rather than pleading, "supplicating" others (men) to act on her behalf. What breaks with custom is not that she wants to impose some private, family laws on the public or the state and to act on behalf of the private, but that she herself wants to act as a public person, that is, to act in the realm of the public and the state.

2.

THEBAN HERALD
Who is the despot of this land? To whom must I announce
the message of Creon who rules over the land of Cadmus,
since Eteocles was slain by the hand of his brother Polyneices,
at the sevenfold gates of Thebes? (*The Suppliants*, 399–402)

THESEUS
You have made a false beginning to your speech,
stranger, in seeking a despot here.
For this city is not ruled by one man, but is free.
The people rule in succession year by year,
allowing no preference to wealth,
but the poor man shares equally with the rich. (*The Suppliants*, 403–408)

The other important point that can be derived from the outlined larger context concerns the question of what exactly the "divine laws" invoked by Antigone refer to. They state that it is wrong to "kill the dead a second time," as Teiresias puts it. These "divine laws," then, are not about the distinction between the public and the private (ancient family traditions) or between our social role and our basic, universal humanity, but about something much more specific: this is precisely about the difference "between two deaths," as Lacan will call it, the realm of the undead. It is about the prohibition of the symbolic murder of a real corpse, or of the exploitation of a corpse as a symbolic stake, its torture and shaming, which in a certain sense precisely *does not acknowledge death*, but imprisons the person far beyond their death, condemning them to "wander without a grave."

So why do we bury the dead and not leave them lying there, "a dinner for the birds and for the dogs," as we read in *Antigone* (206)? I have already quoted Teiresias: *The corpse unburied, robbed of its release.*[3] Why is a human body "released" only when it is properly buried? And released from what? Here, in fact, we touch the foundations of "being human," which, as it turns out, are precisely related to this dimension of (possible) undeadness, to the *capacity to be undead*, one might say. The singularity of the human animal is this dimension of living deadness or dead livingness. What is this dimension and where does it come from?

THEBAN HERALD
You give me here an advantage, as in a game of checkers;
for the city from which I come is ruled
by one man only, not by the mob. (*The Suppliants*, 409–411)

The Herald continues with insults against the political order of Athens, whereupon Theseus develops a real treatise on democracy (equal rights for all, freedom, the public interest, against inequality, against personal appropriation of the Law, against the rule of fear, etc.) (cf. 430–449).

3. The more literal translation would be "unhallowed by funeral rites," but I think this more suggestive, interpretive translation hits the mark in an interesting way, playing nicely on the Christian idea of "releasing the soul." In any case, the idea that the body remains stuck in an inappropriate state if not properly buried is there in both cases.

Let us start answering these questions by pointing out that what is mostly lost in the recent philosophical-realist criticism of the so-called linguistic turn is the precise point at which language is not simply conceived as constitutive of reality and of the way we think about it but is above all something that introduces an additional, *surplus real*. This is a very good encapsulation of what I would call "Lacanian realism." The surplus real is not "constituted through" language; it is more like a parasite on it and on its functioning, with the capacity also to steer it, and our life, in unpredictable directions. In other words, although we can say that this real would not exist if we were not speaking beings, it is not something constituted *by* speech but is essentially its by-product, which is not (directly) assimilable into the symbolic. This surplus real is situated in the intricate topology of the relationship between organic life and the symbolic, with the relationship between death and language as its pivotal point. And, as I shall now try to show via a longer digression into these questions, this is precisely where the importance of funeral rites comes in.

Death is not simply an outer limit of life. And funeral rituals are never simply a way of honoring the deceased, of paying one's last respects and so on, although they are that too. They are a way of making death coincide with itself. For it is this coincidence that finally "releases" a body, allows the deceased to "rest in peace"—and not, for example, to continue to wander and haunt the living. We know that the popular imagination is full of these restless beings, half released and half chained to this place. But why is this necessary? Why does death not naturally, automatically, coincide with itself? Precisely because of the surplus real introduced by speech.

So a first—albeit insufficient—answer would be because, as speaking beings, we have a way of *saying death*, of talking about it, of thinking it, of establishing a relationship to it.[4] It is not obvious to

---

4. I will not repeat the Heideggerian argument here but stick more to what I think is a small but absolutely crucial additional Lacanian twist to the famous Heideggerian being-toward-death.

be able to *say death*—I do not mean the word "death" but what it implies, what it is. How do you say death? That is an interesting paradox: to be able to say death, you have to bring death to life; you have to make it part of life, give it a symbolic existence to which you can relate; you have to resurrect death from death, so to speak. To say death, you have to make it "symbolically alive," alive in the symbolic.

Lacan liked to repeat the Hegelian saying that "the word is the murder of the thing." We could also turn this around or add another twist: the word is the resurrection of a thing that retroactively accomplishes its murder; it is "murder by resurrection." It does not just kill a thing; it kills it by taking it to a different, symbolic life. Moreover, as Slavoj Žižek tellingly noted, the word is the murder of a thing primarily in the sense of its radical dissection; the word "quarters" the thing, tears it out of its embedding in its concrete context, treats its component parts as entities with an autonomous existence: we speak of color, form, shape, and so on as if they possessed self-sufficient being (Žižek 1992, 51).

The symbolic presents us with a strange short circuit, a coincidence of life and death. And it is this insight into the peculiar short circuit of life and death that shapes their relationship, which constitutes the background of the theme that Lacan introduces in various contexts but especially in the seminar *The Ethics of Psychoanalysis* (1997): the theme of the "second death," the difference between two deaths (symbolic and real), and the realm "between two deaths" that plays such a central role in his reading of *Antigone*.

Lacan did not invent this idea—we find it, for example, in the work of the Marquis de Sade, who is also an important reference in the *Ethics* seminar. And just a few years before Lacan conducted this seminar (1959–1960), Ernst Kantorowicz published his famous book *The King's Two Bodies* (2016), which is about a very similar configuration. Take the famous proclamation, "The King is dead. Long live the King!" This is the traditional proclamation made after the accession of a new monarch in various countries. This proclamation of death is an intrinsic and essential part of the inauguration. It signals the continuity of the symbolic mandate, despite or rather—this will be my main argument—*through* the occurrence of death, that is, through discontinuity.

In the Marquis de Sade's work, there is a somewhat different version of the immanent connection between death and the continuation of life. Sade recognizes in their inherent connection the essence of nature and the indestructible life it implies; this, in turn, demands the notion of a "second death" as something that might put an end to this *indestructible life*, which death alone cannot really interrupt. In *Juliette* (in the famous speech by the Pope from the fourth part of the book), we can see clearly the difference between these two deaths: first, there is death as part of the natural cycle of generation and corruption (dying), the constant transformation of nature. All things that die are involved in a new form of life through their corruption; we could say that nature amounts to an absolute "tyranny" of life, the fact that life cannot really be destroyed by death, since death is its immanent moment, itself involved in regeneration, not the opposite of life or its final end. Death is not enough. In the words of the Pope, "At the instant we call death, everything seems to dissolve. . . . But this death is only imaginary, it exists figuratively but in no other way. . . . There is indeed no real death" (Sade 1994, 769–770). Against the background of this impossibility of anything in nature really dying, the idea of an absolute, ultimate crime appears, a crime that would bring about an absolute death, something like a *second death*—a "total destruction," the extinction of the natural cycle itself, thus freeing nature from its own laws, opening the way for the creation of life rather than its reproduction. Reproduction involves and presupposes death, which is why a "second death" would be tantamount to the annihilation of the ability to reproduce.

For Sade, then, this indestructible life is not the opposite of death, but it implies and contains death; and for this very reason, it is indestructible: since death is an integral part of life, it cannot destroy it; it cannot put an end to it. In a sense, we could say that the Sadeian problem is this: How to free death from being merely an internal moment of the regeneration of life? For that, he needs the second death. Normal crimes and forms of destruction are not sufficient for this—they extinguish individual life but not life as such. In other words, the problem of killing, of destroying life, is how to destroy, how to "kill," that which in life is already dead and cannot die. The Sadeian fantasy of absolute annihilation aims, paradoxically, to eliminate death, to render it inoperative.

Sade is very interesting here because his particular obsession can help us to appreciate Lacanian theory in its complexity; it is not reducible to the simple opposition between symbolic and "real"/ empirical life but starts from a singular short circuit between the two, and from a new Real produced in this very same short circuit. The indestructible life that Sade finally wants to destroy, to put an end to, is not simply symbolic life (for example, the "eternal" life in the big Other of memory and historical recognition or a symbolic mandate) but something that can be seen, from a Lacanian perspective, as life that is essentially a *by-product* of the symbolic, its irreducible surplus (which is not itself symbolic). I shall return to this later.

I mentioned Kantorowicz and his book *The King's Two Bodies* and the ritual proclamation after the accession of a new monarch: "The King is dead. Long live the King!"—a formula that points to a continuity of the symbolic mandate, not in spite of but *through* the occurrence of death.[5]

Sticking to the formal aspect for now, we can see a very similar configuration in a very different context: in Lacan's discussion of how sexual reproduction, as a means of perpetuating life (its

5. Kantorowicz's discussion of this formula is, of course, much more complex and, as the title suggests, focuses particularly on the existence of this transcendent, symbolic dimension of the body. For a very forceful contemporary reading of this notion, see Eric Santner's *The Royal Remains* (2011), in which he develops the concept of "flesh" in terms of the bodily dimension of undead, symbolic life, in its relation to the psychoanalytic notion of the drive. I shall also relate this concept to the concept of drive in my further discussion, but let me first dwell a little more on the formal aspect of the central role of death in the continuity of life.

"indestructibility"—in the form of the survival of the species), depends on individual death:

> We know that sexual division, in so far as it reigns over most living beings, is that which ensures the survival of a species. . . . Let us say that the species survives in the form of its individuals. Nevertheless, the survival of the horse as a species has a meaning—each horse is transitory and dies. So you see, the link between sex and death, sex and the death of the individual, is fundamental. (Lacan 1998, 150)

We are dealing here with a very interesting repetition of Kantorowicz's assertion—not in relation to the symbolic mandate, however, but in relation to (sexed) life as such. Life (e.g., of a species) does not continue *despite* the death of individuals but *through it*, with its "help." Death is a necessary condition for the continuity of (sexed) life, a condition for its continuous survival. Life is not indifferent to death; death is its internal moment/condition. We could repeat the aforementioned saying almost verbatim: "The horse is dead. Long live the horse (or long live horses)!"

And of course, it is quite significant that Lacan links this configuration to sexuality (sexual reproduction). The connection he makes here between sex and death has little to do with ideas about the orgasm as a "little death" or with some ecstatic dimension of enjoyment. Rather, it has to do with the *cut in continuity* as an inner moment of that very continuity. Sex—that is to say, sexuation—is first and foremost a cut in the continuity of life, a cut in which something is lost; it is a discontinuity (of life), a loss of life, and, paradoxically, it is the repetition of this cut or loss of life that constitutes the continuity of life, as well as providing the site where the (surplus) enjoyment, *jouissance*, takes place. As such, sex is the point of incidence of death in life.

If we return to Sade for a moment, we can see how this perspective turns the Sadeian fantasy inside out, like a glove; he intends to cover this reproductive cut with the image of torture as a form of ecstatic enjoyment. It is no accident that Sade's obsession with indestructible life takes the form of, if I may put it this way, a fantas-matic *forcing of the sexual* (of enjoyment), which pushes its limit—through torture—to the extremes of the imagination, as if he were trying to make it spit out death, to render death ineffective in its function of ensuring the reproduction and continuity of life. The impossible, unattainable, and yet focal point of total destruction, of absolute death is transposed in the figure of torture into an infinitely prolonged temporality of death, of dying. It is indeed very interesting to see how in *Juliette* the Pope's speech on why murder and killing (as means of death) are the most natural things on Earth transitions almost imperceptibly to, and concludes with, a long list of tortures known from history. This transition from a "simple" killing or mur-der to torture transforms the instantaneity of death into a scene of its possibly infinite duration. It transforms temporality into a spatial category. Torture is a way of living one's death and rendering it in-operative (as a point of reproduction); it is a fantasmatic freezing of death that removes it from the cycle of reproduction. Death is drawn out into torture and thereby becomes properly ecstatic, "displaced from its proper place," as the etymology of the Greek term *ekstasis* suggests. In other words, it becomes the *scene* of an impossible, infinite enjoyment, multiplied and enhanced by mortal agony, rather than obliterated by it. This is the essence of the Sadeian fantasmatic theater. The victims are tortured endlessly, beyond all limits of imagi-nation, yet they continue to live and suffer, even becoming more and more beautiful, as if endowed with another, sublime body.

But—to return to Lacan—it seems that in his version of the intrin-sic relation between life and death involved in sexual division/repro-duction, we have (surprisingly!) lost the symbolic and the language that we started with and that Lacan is supposed to be all about. Do the two configurations (the continuity of a symbolic mandate and the continuity of the organic life of a species since both presuppose death) simply mirror each other? Is it the *analogy* that constitutes their relationship, or is there a more fundamental connection to be found between the two?

Immediately following the passage quoted earlier that links sexual division/reproduction to death, Lacan goes on to say that the elementary structures of *social/symbolic* functioning and their fundamental combinatory operations are inseparably related to sexual reality, to copulation, because the fulcrum of reproduction (and its implication of death) is found here. Let us quote this extremely important—and conceptually very bold—passage in its entirety:

> Existence, thanks to sexual division, rests upon copulation, accentuated in two poles that time-honoured tradition has tried to characterize as the male pole and the female pole. This is because the mainspring of reproduction is to be found there. Around this fundamental reality, there have always been grouped, harmonized, other characteristics, more or less bound up with the finality of reproduction. I can do no more than point out here, what, in the biological register, is associated with sexual differentiation, in the form of secondary sexual characteristics and functions. We know today how, in society, a whole distribution of functions in a play of alternation is grounded on this terrain. It is modern structuralism that has brought this out best, by showing that it is at the level of matrimonial alliance, as opposed to natural generation, to biological lineal descent—at the level therefore of the signifier—that the fundamental exchanges take place and it is there that we find once again that the most elementary structures of social functioning are inscribed in the terms of a combinatory.
>
> The integration of this combinatory into sexual reality raises the question of whether it is not in this way that the signifier came into the world, into the world of man.
>
> What would make it legitimate to maintain that it is through sexual reality that the signifier came into the world—that man learnt to think—is the recent field of discoveries that begins by a more accurate study of mitosis. (Lacan 1998, 150–151)

Here we have a bold assertion that posits a primordial coincidence of sexuality and signifier, of sexual reality and symbolic reality. Lacan is still wavering at this point in his teaching, and in the next paragraph he retreats from this explicit assertion by suggesting an "analogical" relationship between the two. But in the preceding passage we have this suggestion quite explicitly on the table: the signifier came into the world through sexual reality and sexual division due to the latter's involvement in reproduction, a reproduction that includes death (a loss of life) as its internal moment. The structure of the signifier begins with a *minus*, a subtraction, as it is involved in sexual reproduction and transmitted, passed on, through it.

I should say, in passing, if we take this claim seriously, we can ask ourselves what happens when and if sexual reality is completely decoupled from procreation (reproduction), from the continuity of life. Obviously, practices like birth control or even artificial insemination cannot do this, since they merely make a separation between sexual enjoyment, or simply the act of copulation, and reproduction. Yet reproduction itself, even if it is "artificial," remains sexual, even when it is decoupled from the life that produces sexual cells. Cloning has so far been the only attempt to actually circumvent sexual reproduction, suggesting an eventual possibility that humans could reproduce in ways other than sexually. If this, or something similar stemming from new technological advances, were to work and become the primary means of reproduction, it would perhaps make sense to ask what the implications would be for the symbolic order: Would this imply a completely different symbolic horizon or perhaps even the end of the symbolic order as such? We could also ask another question: Could the essence of language, implicit in its functioning, change completely? Or would we just lose the link to that negativity through which the signifier came into the word and started its combinatory game?

But let us return to our original question and to Lacan from *Seminar XI*—he makes a further, even more crucial suggestion, which is directly related to our discussion: death is represented in speaking beings not simply or only by signifiers, such as words referring to dying and death or by words as such (which always involve the murder of a thing), but also, and perhaps primarily, by the *drive*. As I have already pointed out in my brief discussion of Sade, the "indestructible life" does not refer to what is called symbolic life (such as the life of my name or reputation or symbolic mandate, which will live on when I die); it does not simply refer to the (supposedly indestructible) life of the symbolic sign or "signifier" that represents me. Reputations, after all, are always destructible and have always been regarded as such, which is why such attention is devoted to their maintenance. In contrast to this strange indestructible life, symbolic life seems very fragile, precarious, easily destroyed, annihilated. There is nothing simply eternal or indestructible about the symbolic. If anything, it is precisely and only in the symbolic that it is possible to bring about a radical erasure, a clear cut, a beginning ex nihilo. As for "indestructible life," it appears primarily through this other image, the image of eternal regeneration and its pulsating movement, which seems to follow its course no matter what we do or what happens; it appears as something that *cannot be interrupted* ("killed") in any way. And it is this impossibility that, in Sade, requires the perspective, the "fantasy," of a radical, absolute crime that he conceives and the perspective of a second death. This something that is impossible to kill because of its intrinsic relation to death also has many other images or figures, especially in modern pop culture: for example, that of the undead or the living dead. Žižek has written extensively about this figure.

We could simply put it this way: there are two sides to the symbolic. There is symbolic life (mandate, signifier, and the autonomous existence of a certain aspect of the thing in that signifier), and then there is this undeadness, the undead life that seems to come with it, accompanying it as an unexpected (and somehow unwelcome) bonus. They are not the same. As speaking creatures, human beings participate not only in symbolic life but also in fate, in the state of undeadness that comes with the symbolic but is not reducible to it and that, according to psychoanalysis, is the very fulcrum of human sexuality—and is related to the drives. Sex is thus the occurrence of both death and an unexpected surplus of life, which are inseparable.

This is precisely what the term "death drive" refers to in the context of Lacanian psychoanalysis: it refers to the way in which an irreducible surplus life (surplus-enjoyment) emerges and exists as the flip side of symbolic life, clinging to it and often tipping it in strange, unpredictable directions. This surplus does not exist outside the symbolic, but it is neither itself symbolic nor covered by the symbolic; it is not "symbolic life" in any usual sense of the term. This is the other, "shadowy" side of symbolic life as the "eternal," independent, autonomous life of the signifier: it is like its underpinning. It is not directly part of a symbolic chain; it is its undercurrent. Freud, in discussing the drives, spoke of a "constant force" (Freud 2001, 119), a form of pressure. Lacan developed this notion at length (as one of the four fundamental concepts of psychoanalysis) and linked it, among other things, to the idea of the pulsating circuit, a constant *returning to the circuit* of reproduction—this time not of life but of a surplus satisfaction (that is to say, a different one than that of an organic need). Significantly, the word Lacan opts for in French to translate Freud's *Treib*, hitherto translated as "instinct," is *pulsion*.[6] "If the drive may be satisfied without attaining what, from the point of view of a biological totalization of function, would be the satisfaction of its end of reproduction, it is because it is a partial drive [i.e., it has attained surplus satisfaction], and its aim is simply this return into circuit" (Lacan 1998, 179).

All this forms the background of Lacan's colorful explanation of what the fantasy of indestructible life relates to in the Real: he famously introduces at this point the image of an intangible, "false" organ and calls it the *lamella*.

> The lamella is something extra-flat, which moves like the amoeba. It is just a little more complicated. But it goes everywhere. And as it is something—I will tell you shortly why—that is related to what the sexed being loses in sexuality, it is, like the amoeba in relation to sexed beings, immortal—because it survives any division, any scissiparous intervention. And it can run around.

6. Whereas the English translation moved from "instinct" to "drive."

Well! This is not very reassuring. But suppose it comes and envelops your face while you are quietly asleep. I can't see how we would not join battle with a being capable of these properties. But it would not be a very convenient battle. This lamella, this organ, whose characteristic is not to exist, but which is nevertheless an organ . . . is the libido.

It is the libido, *qua* pure life instinct, that is to say, immortal life, or irrepressible life, life that has need of no organ, simplified, indestructible life. It is precisely what is subtracted from the living being by virtue of the fact that it is subject to the cycle of sexed reproduction. And it is of this that all the forms of the *objet a* that can be enumerated are the representatives, the equivalents. The *objets a* are merely its representatives, its figures. (Lacan 1998, 197–198)

This is a very important and dense passage. It is constructed around the difference between amoeboid beings (nonindividuated beings who survive division because there is no loss/minus/death involved) and sexual beings, for whom division, which is at work in reproduction, involves a minus, a loss (even at the chromosomal level), death; and this minus or loss links reproduction, as a continuity of life, to death. So here we again encounter the idea of the connection between sex and death, between sex and the death of the individual as inscribed in the survival of the species.

And the drive or libido appears as *the return* (return via "march of the signifiers") of that which "is subtracted from the living being by . . . the cycle of sexual reproduction." The (mythical) immortal, *irrepressible life*, being by definition lost, returns as something more accurately called *undead life*, something indestructible because it is undead (libido, the drive). Better yet, this mythical irrepressible life instinct exists in reality only as the death drive: not a drive aiming at death but the drive to repeat the surplus(-enjoyment) that occurs at the point of the cut/loss involved in sexual division. The death drive is essentially related to surplus-enjoyment, which emerges in the process of the death drive circling around something that is not there. In this context, Lacan also points to the rim-like structure of erogenous zones, their affinity with cuts, edges, openings in the structure of the body (Lacan 1998, 168).

And this is precisely the point at which the Freudian opposition between the life drive, or *Lebenstrieb* (also called the "sex drive"), and the death drive, or *Todestrieb*, becomes untenable from the Lacanian perspective. They are one and the same.

> The relation to the Other is precisely that which, for us, brings out what is represented by the lamella—not sexed polarity, the relation between masculine and feminine, but the relation between the living subject and that which he loses by having to pass, for his reproduction, through the sexual cycle. In this way I explain the essential affinity of every drive with the zone of death, and reconcile the two sides of the drive—which, at one and the same time, makes present sexuality in the unconscious and represents, in its essence, death. (Lacan 1998, 199)

It is important to note that death is thus "represented" as and by this undead, *surplus* life (surplus-enjoyment) and not by some kind of abysmal nothingness. It is not a void that represents death but the mere presence of libidinal sexuality. Or, as I have already indicated, death is represented in speaking beings not only or simply by signifiers, by words referring to dying and death, but also and perhaps primarily by the drive, by the very ex-sistence—and insistence—of the drive. For this very reason, every drive is essentially a death drive. The drive and its modes of satisfaction are disturbing. Death is "represented" in our lives by something that always disturbs it, from within.

This idea also involves an important point that Lacan makes in relationship to Heidegger and his *Sein-zum-Tode*, being-toward-death, which defines the human difference for Heidegger (i.e., what makes us human).[7] What is the status of death in Heidegger's being-toward-death? If death is not basically trivial, this is for the simple reason that our awareness and relationship/attitude to it make all the difference and open up the metaphysical dimension proper. To put it very

---

7. I am repeating and summarizing here a longer argument that I developed in *What Is Sex?*

simply, because of death, it matters how we are and live, what we do. Žižek was right to point out, in this context, how it would be wrong to read the "being-toward-death" and, more generally, the theme of human finitude in contemporary philosophy simply as a morbid obsession with what makes humanity equal to and thus reduced to a mere animal, to read it as blindness to that properly metaphysical dimension that eventually allows us to gain "immortality" in a specifically human way. This kind of reading ignores a crucial point made by Heidegger apropos of Kant's critical break: the very space for the specific "immortality" in which human beings can eventually participate is opened up by humankind's unique relationship to finitude and the possibility of death. What is thus at stake (with this theme of "finitude" and being-toward-death) is not that it denies the specifically human mode of "immortality"; rather, it reminds us that this "immortality" (things and deeds irreducible to mere survival) is based precisely on the specific mode of human finitude (Žižek 1999, 163).

Where this question is concerned, there is no doubt that Lacan belongs to the post-Kantian perspective as formulated by Heidegger. The shift (and, with it, a significant difference with respect to Heidegger) occurs at another point, and the simplest way to formulate it is perhaps as follows: the structural place occupied, in Heidegger, by the idea of death made possible by language becomes, with Lacan, the Real of enjoyment, *jouissance*, its relentless persecution of us, so to speak. They are both related to language but not in the same way or on the same level.

Lacan's point here is extremely precise and at the same time far-reaching: it is not simply our attitude toward (the possibility of) death that opens up the space of the specifically human dimension (for example, the possibility of actions that are not reducible to the causality of the positive order of Being, to this or that calculation of pleasures); rather, it is the fact that we are situated within an (unsought) portion of enjoyment that makes different attitudes toward death possible to begin with. Death as such, in itself, does not yet involve the possibility of a "dramatic" relationship to itself;

this relationship becomes "dramatic" only when *jouissance* intervenes: "The dialogue of life and death . . . becomes dramatic only from that moment when enjoyment intervenes in the equilibrium of life and death. The vital point, the point where . . . a speaking being emerges is this disturbed [*dérangé*] relationship to one's own body which is called *jouissance*" (Lacan 2011, 43). The disturbed relationship to one's own body: this is where the representation of death, how it affects the way we live, comes into play. It is enjoyment, then, related to the drive, that breaks open the (supposedly) closed circle of animal life and awakens us to metaphysics, to ideas, to thinking, to principles and ethical attitudes.[8]

Lacan's attitude to language is extremely interesting here and could be summarized as follows: *because of language, death is represented not only in or through language* but also and fundamentally through a disturbing, undead excess of life. Language is not reducible (back) to language. This is what new realist ontologies often overlook: it is because of language that another, additional, nonlinguistic Real exists in the universe.

This, then—to recapitulate—would be the predicament that constitutes both the tragedy and the comedy of humans as beings of language: we live (exist) in the symbolic while being *undead* in the Real (neither dead nor alive but undead—this is where the death drive is located, both conceptually and topologically). This state of being undead is the effect, a kind of unsought bonus, of the symbolic and its murder of the Thing.

We can now return to the starting point of this long digression: the question of funeral rites. Funeral rites constitute a symbolic ritual aimed precisely at appeasing, "containing," this other, undead life of

---

8. Enjoyment is usually put down as something that intoxicates us, sedates us, dulls us. But Lacan makes the opposite claim, or perhaps a claim that is on a more fundamental level: enjoyment (unlike pleasure) is something that awakens us and opens up an additional path of human engagement. The latter may, of course, include intoxication and sedation, but paradoxically, these are possible only against the background of, and in response to, a more fundamental awakening.

the subject. Funeral rites are there to make this undead life coincide with the empirical life of the subject, to allow the disturbing undead life also to die, to rest. We are undead in many ways throughout our lives—while we are alive, our lives "contain" and frame this undeadness and are driven by it. When we die, and no symbolic ritual is performed, all that remains is this undead life, no longer held by anything but holding "us" as prisoners of its blind persistence; we turn into it, even into Stephen King's *It*. And this seems to be one of the most persistent images that haunt the human imagination.

This is why the refusal of a proper burial has always been considered the most severe, drastic punishment. In the Christian tradition, it is synonymous with eternal damnation: being condemned to eternal *restlessness* (instead of being able to "rest in peace") and in that state haunting the living. Indeed, this undead restlessness seems even more terrible than the torments of Hell, although they are not independent of each other. We see here how the problem of human life and its "finitude" is never simply death: one wishes to die, but one cannot even die completely. Once we are dead, it is not simply "we" who must be told to "rest in peace"; it is the (death) drive.

Funeral rites are supposed to regulate this excess, to appease it, to give it a framework—as if the symbolic recognition of death and the dead (funeral rites) were there to accomplish, finally, the full exchange of life and death, their *separation*, the one ceding its place to the other, without that nasty shadowy supplement of undeadness that the symbolic brings with it. Funeral rites perform a disconnection of life and death, their short-circuiting or mutual implication, releasing the body from the grip of the symbolic. We are "dead" when life finally coincides with itself, without this additional, disturbing play of plus and minus, without this supplement. In this sense, funeral rites are symbolic rituals that paradoxically aim to undo precisely the (side) effect of the symbolic.

If the refusal of a proper burial constitutes a kind of intentionally inflicted undeadness, there exists yet another configuration in which undeadness (a "return of the living dead") is a result, a symptom of *failed* funeral rites, in a broader sense of a failed integration of a traumatic event into the symbolic.

> The "return of the living dead" is . . . the reverse of the proper funeral rite. While the latter implies a certain reconciliation, an acceptance of loss, the return of the dead signifies that they cannot find their proper place in the text of tradition. The two great traumatic events of the holocaust and the gulag are, of course, exemplary cases of the return of the dead in the twentieth century. The shadows of their victims will continue to chase us as "living dead" until we give them a decent burial, until we integrate the trauma of their death into our historical memory. (Žižek 1992, 23)

From the perspective of this configuration, traumatic events are as such producers of the "living dead": they create and introduce into the (subjective and collective) world the dimension of the undead in the form of an unbindable excess that constitutes the core of any trauma. The two configurations are not the same, although they imply the same elements: the first condemns us to the state of undeadness, whereas the second condemns us to be haunted by the undead as the excessive surplus constituted by trauma.

We can see how, in *Antigone*, the two configurations actually overlap: the traumatic event of the two brothers killing each other (which can also be seen as a prolongation of the traumatic dimension of Oedipus's reign) is further aggravated by Creon's curious attempt to integrate this trauma into the symbolic (into the historical memory of Thebes) by refusing one of the brothers funeral rites: a strange attempt to integrate the traumatic excess into the symbolic by symbolically excluding it from it, that is, by redoubling the exclusion. This, we could say, is why it returns in the Real with vengeance, flaring up in the center of the tragedy with Antigone and her own traumatic undeadness. Creon's refusal to have Polyneices properly buried, and thus to punish him beyond usual human punishment, is not there only as the trigger that sets Antigone off (and hence "explains" the development of the story). The dimension "between two deaths," the notion of the undead, is as such at the very center of the play; it is Antigone herself who enacts it as her destiny, albeit in the opposite sense, that of being *buried alive*.

Moreover, and more generally speaking, the issue of the noncoincidence of life with itself, the discrepancy between real and symbolic life, is very much at stake throughout the entire Theban trilogy. Oedipus becomes Oedipus (that is to say, everything we associate with that name) because he starts out as symbolically dead: he is thought, and presumed, dead. His killing his father, his marrying his mother, his conceiving Antigone, Polyneices, Eteocles, Ismene—all this happens from within this strange realm of him being symbolically dead (symbolically nonexistent) yet still very much alive. And then a strange thing happens at the end of *Oedipus the King*: when everything comes out, and Oedipus's actions are (retrospectively) revealed as hideous crimes, Oedipus refuses to kill himself; he refuses—we could say—to take the opportunity to finally synchronize his symbolic death with his real death, appeasing the unrest that comes with their divergence. In a sense, Oedipus refuses his own funeral. Instead he chooses the life of the outcast, of the undead surplus of life, and refuses to subjectivize himself in the figure of guilt.

When at the end of *Oedipus the King* Oedipus emerges from Jocasta's chambers (she has just killed herself), blood dripping from his face (he has just blinded himself), things become really interesting in this respect. He says, roughly, "Curse on the man who . . . stole me from death and saved me," *condemning me to a still greater misfortune. Without this man, I would never have come to kill my father or to sleep with my mother.* He goes on: "If there is any ill worse than ill, that is the lot of Oedipus" (*Oedipus the King*, 1351, 1365–1366).

The leader of the Chorus, who quickly agrees with Oedipus that it would have been better for him to die immediately after his birth, takes the occasion to say, in effect, *Indeed, what are you still doing here alive, given that you had the perfect opportunity and excuse to end your life beside the body of Jocasta? "You would be better dead,* he says, *than blind and living"* (*Oedipus the King,* 1368). It is certainly surprising that Oedipus himself does not come to this same heroic conclusion. "Better dead than blind and living": the beauty and ambiguity of this remark by the Chorus come from the fact that it refers, at one and the same time, to the moment of the play when it is pronounced (Oedipus would have done better to kill himself instead of blinding himself) *and* to Oedipus's past (it would have been better if Oedipus had died right after he was born; if he had never lived, he would never have blindly committed his scandalous deeds). In sum, Oedipus has always been blind; he has been blind his entire life—but then, when he finally gained the power of sight, when he saw what he had done, he tore out his eyes, declaring, *I prefer to continue being blind!* Thus Oedipus responds to the Chorus with harsh words: *Don't lecture me,* he exclaims, and he adds that he does not have the slightest desire to go directly to Hades, where he would once again have to see his father and his mother.

This tone may strike us as unsuitable for a hero. Instead of taking his symbolic debts upon himself and "settling" them with his death, Oedipus begins to quibble, to protest, even to haggle: he finds the price excessive; he is the victim of an injustice. This element of the drama is emphasized even more in *Oedipus at Colonus,* where it expands to fill the entire play.

Indeed, the fact that Oedipus does not die at the end of the play warrants further attention. At the very least we can say that this is an atypical ending for a tragedy, because it seems to interfere with the mechanism of catharsis. If Oedipus had died, his parricide and incest would have remained the central Thing, around which Oedipus's image and tragic destiny would have erected a fascinating screen to arrest and capture our desire. But instead, what happens in the case of Oedipus is that Oedipus himself becomes the Thing of his tragedy, the outcast, "a thing of guilt and holy dread so great it appalls the earth, the rain from heaven, the light of day," as Creon generously describes him, this time in Robert Fagles's translation (*Oedipus the King,* 1561–1563 [Sophocles 1982]). There is no sublime image (not even one of suffering) at the end of *Oedipus the King.* Oedipus's is an undead life that won't go away.

Not only does Oedipus not die at the end of *Oedipus the King,* but he also appears as the principal character of the "sequel," *Oedipus at Colonus,* which, we might say, immortalizes his life as a blind outcast. Antigone is the one who accompanies him there; she becomes his "eyes," stays with him until he (rather mysteriously) dies. And, incidentally, Oedipus also has no (known) grave; he simply vanishes without a trace (evoking, in a sense, the Sphinx's disappearance after Oedipus solves her riddle in *Oedipus the King*).

This is not all. The quandary of the relationship between the symbolic and the real lies at the very heart of Oedipus's (unconscious) crimes. It raises questions such as, What makes a father a father? What makes a mother a mother?

Here, it is very instructive to see what Oedipus (at Colonus) says about his parricide in his dialog with Creon, who at some point wants to bring Oedipus back to Thebes—since a new oracle has predicted prosperity to the town where Oedipus is buried—but Oedipus refuses to come. What makes this dialog particularly captivating is that the two speakers address a third person, Theseus (King of Athens), and a chorus of Athenians. Creon wants to persuade the Athenians that Oedipus is a truly repugnant criminal to whom they should refuse hospitality and who should be handed over to him, Creon. As for Oedipus, who doesn't want to leave, he must convince the Athenians that this is not true, that he is not in fact a criminal. Thus, from the dramaturgical point of view, this dialog is central, since it presents us with a situation in which a kind of big Other—a "jury"—must decide whether Oedipus is in fact a criminal.

Of course, Creon does not hesitate to use harsh words and accusations: "an unholy man, a parricide, a man with whom his mother had been found!" (*Oedipus at Colonus,* 944–945). *I would never have thought,* he says to Theseus and his men, *that you, most honorable Athenians, would do anything but condemn such a wretched man.* Oedipus responds to this, also addressing himself to

the Athenians, with an argument worthy of a skillful lawyer addressing a jury:

> Just answer me one thing:
> if someone tried to kill you here and now,
> you righteous gentlemen, what would you do,
> inquire first if the stranger was your father?
> Or would you not first try to defend yourself? (*Oedipus at Colonus*,
> 991–995)

Evidently, the same argument works equally well for the incest: Are
you in the habit of asking a woman, before you sleep with her, if she
might, by any chance, be your mother?

The comic effect of this reply, with which Oedipus conquers the
hearts of the Athenians, must not divert us from the real point at which
it aims: *What is a father?* How does one recognize a father? And if I am
not capable of recognizing someone as my father (and he, for his part,
is equally incapable of recognizing me), is he still a father?[9]

With all this in mind, let us return to *Antigone*, the play. I was discussing earlier the Sadeian obsession with regeneration and its
impossible interruption. And speaking of Antigone, it is worth not-
ing that her name (at least in one of its etymologies) means "against
progeny": against having children, against regeneration—as if evoking, already in name, the radical break related to the notion of the
second death.

But, seen from another angle, the realm "between two deaths"
appears above all to be something of an obsession for Creon. With
Polyneices and his punishment, he seems to aim at exposing his not
so much bare life as "bare death," refusing to (symbolically) declare

9. See also: "If Oedipus is a whole man, if Oedipus doesn't have an Oedipus complex, it
is because in his case there is no father at all. The person who served as father was his adop-
tive father. And, my good friends, that's the case with all of us, because as the Latin has it,
pater est quem justae nuptiae demonstrant, that is to say, the father is he who acknowledges
us" (Lacan 1997, 309).

the dead dead, leaving him in a disturbing undead state in which his body remains hostage, prisoner of a restless undeadness, of the undead-life. "The corpse unburied, robbed of its release." Burial releases the body from its undead passions. It also symbolically interrupts the inexorable cycle of regeneration. It would be interesting in this context to interrogate the significance of the *vault* as, among other things, a peculiar place that, with its stone walls, prevents the putrefying flesh from "feeding" life in general, becoming an immediate part of it, of its regenerative cycle. The vault, the tombstone, but also the coffin, to some extent, all figure as symbolic markers of interruption in the continuity of life. To mark, and hence honor, this interruption (death) is thus a way of honoring an *individual* life, subjectivized life, as opposed to life in general. An individual, subjective life can be honored, affirmed—and in this way made "immortal"—by means of recognizing its death, its mortality, not by disregarding it. Subjective immortality depends on this cut. A vault or a tombstone provides it. Its long-lasting material resists death and destruction, yet it also lastingly testifies, declares, that death has taken place and hence that *there has been individual life*, with its possibly immortal achievements.

We could thus say that Polyneices's uncovered, rotting body is the embodiment, the emblem, of the undead surplus, the existence of which the *whole of Oedipus's family* is fatally made to tarry with, in different ways. And what happens in *Antigone* is that with her demand and her perseverance, she *sublimates* this undead surplus: this *Unding*, to use a very appropriate German word. She sublimates it by her actions, which lead her to end up buried alive, embodying a "buried life" (as we can read in the play). Polyneices's is a death that cannot die; Antigone's becomes a life that cannot be lived alive (sustained), yet it liberates life, generating a sublime image of its traumatic surplus. It is this image that Lacan relates to Antigone as figure of "pure desire," desire in its pure state (beyond all particular, "pathological" objects), desire as subjectivation of the impossible Thing—a blindingly "white desire," as Bernard Baas has beautifully put it (1992).

Sublimation is an important notion in Lacan's *Ethics* seminar, in which it receives its most famous, albeit not the last, definition: to sublimate is to *elevate something* (an object) *to the dignity of the Thing*. In Antigone's case, we could say that she elevates "the Oedipal abject" (*Unding*) to the dignity of the Thing (*das Ding*). With her actions, Antigone immortalizes, glorifies (or should we perhaps say "petrifies," raises a stone monument to?) the disturbing undead, blind drive of Oedipus, which *reemerges*, thanks to Creon, in the abject undeadness of Polyneices; she immortalizes it by elevating it into a most singular and blinding appearance of an absolute desire, sustaining all by itself the difference between two deaths. And here we come to an interesting paradox, question: How to relate or reconcile Antigone as embodying a radical cut, interruption, End (of regeneration, a "second death"), with the idea that she "immortalizes the family *átē*," as Lacan puts it? How to think together a radical End (disappearance) and immortality, even infinity?

In Joan Copjec's book on sublimation and femininity (*Imagine There's No Woman: Ethics and Sublimation*), she provides a most interesting answer, which starts by reminding us of Claude Lefort's discussion of how "immortality" appears in the modern age. This discussion is most pertinent, not only because it shows why Antigone can appear as a prominently *modern* figure (as she certainly does) but also because it brings together several key notions and relations that I have been discussing so far: the gap and the relationship between the individual and the species, the notion of singularity and its relation to the universal, and the notion of sublimation. Here is a brief outline of Copjec's reading of these issues.

In the essay "The Death of Immortality?" (1988), Lefort describes the change that the classical notion of immortality underwent in modernity. As Copjec sums up his argument, the modern notion of immortality benefits from the collapse of our belief in the timeless realm of eternity.

> Where formerly every deed (and the active life, in general) was
> thought to fail insofar as it was unable to elevate itself *out of time*,

into eternity, in modernity the deed was reconceived as affording one
the possibility of transcending historical time *within* time. This is what
is new: this idea that the act could raise itself out of impotence, or out
of the immanence of its historical conditions, without raising itself
out of time. It is at this point that the act—or work in this specific
sense—took on a value it could not have had in the classical era.
The valorization of the act helped to forge, Lefort argues, a new
link between immortality and the "sense of posterity."
(Copjec 2002, 20)

Crucial in this account is the emphasis on the recognition, the affirma-
tion, of a cut (implied in an act), an interruption, a break, as constituting the very bridge or link to posterity and durability. Take the
example of the great social revolutions at the end of the eighteenth
century: they may have severed all ties with the past, "but they did so,
paradoxically, in order to establish a permanence in time, a durability of human deeds that was not possible previously. The difference
arises because the 'sense of posterity' now took place across a historical *break*" (Copjec 2002, 20–21).

Copjec very perceptively contrasts Lefort's with another modern
discussion of immortality: Hans Blumenberg's (from his *The Legitimacy of the Modern Age*, 1985). Blumenberg follows the Feuerbachian argument that in modernity the notion of immortality
basically appears as an attempt to heal the wound between the
species and the individual: it is not an individual human being but
only a species that can "accomplish the destiny of man." Immortality could belong only to the species as a whole; yet since the species can never appear as a whole, the notion of immortality is in fact
a way of negating history in order to posit a spatial beyond where
the future is already waiting to bestow itself on the individual: it is
mistaken, because it unjustifiably converts some as-yet-unrealized
temporal progress (of the species) into a "spatial paradise," a kind
of totality of infinite progress. This is what makes Blumenberg
follow the Feuerbachian suggestion that we should simply give up
the notion of immortality as erroneous, as something that can have
no place in modernity.

The difference between the two modern perspectives on the question of immortality clearly reiterates the conceptual difference between actual infinity and bad infinity (defined as infinite progress toward an unattainable point). Whereas the latter implies a sheer and continuous succession of individuals, none of whom possesses or actualizes immortality, the former involves a paradoxical notion of an "immortal individual." Yet this individual immortality presupposes and is possible only on the basis of a radical break and discontinuity: that is to say, of a "second death."[10] And it is not difficult to see how the figure of Antigone fits perfectly this specific modern notion of immortality—which can in turn go a long way toward explaining her explosive (re)appearance and presence in modernity. Antigone's figure becomes emblematic of the modern notion of the Act (ethical act, political act) as something capable of retroactively changing the very conditions of *its* possibility and so affecting the set of possibilities that define the space into which it intervenes.

There is more: Lefort further links this notion of immortality to that of singularity: "The sense of immortality proves to be bound up with the conquest of a place *which cannot be taken*, which is invulnerable, because it is the place of someone . . . who, by accepting all that is most singular in his life, refuses to submit to the coordinates of space and time and who . . . for us . . . is not dead" (Lefort 1988, 279). Someone dies, leaving behind his place, which outlives him and is unfillable by anyone else. As Copjec points out, this idea constructs a specific notion of the social, whereby it is conceived to consist not only *of* particular individuals and their relations to each other but also *as* relation to these unoccupiable places. "If, with the collapse of eternity, the modern world is not decimated by historical time, it is because this unoccupiable place, this sense of singularity, somehow knots it together in time. Singularity itself, that which appears

10. We could say that Blumenberg lacks precisely this notion of the second death (a death that is not simply biological), which arises from the recognition of an intrinsic entanglement of life and death.

most to disperse society, is here posited as essential rather than antagonistic to a certain modern social bond" (Copjec 2002, 23). On the basis of Lefort's mention of "the writer" in this context, Copjec makes a further point: it is the psychoanalytic concept of sublimation that can clarify how singularity is able to figure and not be effaced by the social bond. In other words, Copjec argues that it is the notion of sublimation that can bridge this gap between singularity and sociality: in other words, sublimation has the capacity to link the singular with the universal.

Indeed, in the context of *Antigone*, all this resonates in a powerful and multiple way: she "immortalizes" the family *átē* by binding it irrevocably to her own mortal individuality: that is to say, her own singular act of interrupting, breaking, all ties with her world. Attaching herself entirely to the unburied, rotting body of her brother, she attracts the gazes that would normally turn away from it and makes them follow her in her singular destiny, as if wrapping the rotting body and its undead life in her act and her destiny. In a way, she does bury Polyneices: she buries him in the empty space held open, forcefully, by the absolute desire that sustains her actions and her perseverance. She buries him not to hide his rotting body from our eyes but *for all of us* to see it, forever, as the undead, excessive core of her sublime image.

"I'D LET THEM ROT"

With Antigone, things are always simultaneously very singular (not to say personal) yet very general, principled; and the time has come to include in our discussion what seems to be the most particular and peculiar feature of her claim, which relates to the singular "family business" that lies at the center of the whole trilogy. We know that Freud has made of this criminal family's singularity a general ground of what is considered normalcy. He made on the basis of Oedipus's family a statement on family in general, in spite of the fact—or perhaps, rather, on the basis of the fact?—that Oedipus's family is pretty much the most dysfunctional family one can imagine, as Mladen Dolar once put it (2009).[1]

1. To rerun the whole story once more, Oedipus (unknowingly) kills his father and marries his own mother, with whom he has four children: Antigone, Ismene, Polyneices, and Eteocles. When he finds out what he has done (at the end of *Oedipus the King*), he does not kill himself (as everybody expects, even encourages, him to do) but gouges his eyes out and "chooses" the life of an exile. Antigone accompanies him, whereas his two sons remain in Thebes fighting each other for the succession. When he is about to die (at the end of *Oedipus at Colonus*), Oedipus curses his sons (and particularly Polyneices), predicting that they will

So the question seems to be this: Is it a really dysfunctional family? Or, rather, is it the other, undead side of every normal, functional family, as Freud would seem to suggest? I started by evoking a dimension of the "unfamiliar" that surrounds the figure of Antigone, which we could now directly relate to the issue of *family* and work our way to the unfamiliar, uncanny point of family and familiarity as such.

The moment has come to look at what is probably the most famous, and infamous, controversial passage of *Antigone*, in which the heroine tries to explain why she is doing what she is doing: persisting in her claim, defying Creon and his decree, regardless of consequences. Here is the passage:

> Were I a mother, with children or husband dead,
> I'd let them molder.[2] I should not have chosen
> in such a case to cross the state's decree.
> What is the law that lies behind these words?
> One husband gone, I might have found another,
> or a child form a new man in first child's place,
> but with my parents covered up in death,
> no brother for me, ever, could be born.
> Such was the law by which I honored you. (*Antigone*, 905–914)

This is the key to, as well as a truly strange explanation of, what she is doing and why she is doing it. It seems to directly contradict, even belie, many readings, particularly readings that insist on any kind of universal humanity that Antigone is supposedly defending by her stance and her actions: the universal humanity of even the worst criminals, on account of which everybody deserves a burial. Perhaps everybody does indeed deserve a burial, but here's the rub: Antigone wouldn't do it for everybody. She wouldn't do it for her children. She wouldn't do it for her husband. She would only do it for a brother

---

die at each other's hand. Before leaving his father with this curse on him, Polyneices makes Antigone promise to give him a proper burial.

2. In the title, I took the liberty of substituting the term "rot" for "molder." The Greek term is *tékō*.

and only because their parents are already dead, so she can't have another brother. There is something rather *outrageous* about this. What kind of argument is it? If your child dies, you can have another; if your husband dies, you can marry another. We talk a lot these days about the commodification of our relationships, but this kind of direct language is still shocking.

It is most interesting how purely symbolic ties, not any kind of affection or attachment, define this claim. It is about a (bio)*logical* impossibility, not about individual uniqueness. If she could have another brother, Polyneices rotting out there would not be a problem (implying something like "a brother is a brother," just like "a child is a child"—as long as you can have another). Kinship is not the reason for her actions (she does not do it *because* he was her brother) but something else: it is almost as if she is trying to patch up a hole in the structure of kinship or as if that *particular* hole in the structure of kinship was especially unbearable, charged with something far beyond what it actually is. This may explain—or, rather, cast in a different light—the icy coldness of her claim and of the calculation behind it.

So why Polyneices? We could perhaps say that everybody is replaceable, but not all people are *reproducible*. But is this really about reproduction, regeneration, or, rather, about properly acknowledging, honoring its end: its *dead end*, we might say?

There is something about Antigone and her brother(s) that involves a singular twist, something that is—pardon the expression—particularly *screwed*. Let us remember that Antigone actually had three, not only two, brothers, one of whom also happened to be her father. Her father, Oedipus, the original criminal of the Theban saga, was at the same time her brother. And this same brother, who was also her father, cursed Polyneices in front of Antigone and predicted his death at his brother Eteocles's hand (in *Oedipus at Colonus*). There is something about brothers—and about the kinship caught in a strange loop between the biological and the symbolic—that for Antigone cannot be separated from the incest or from incest and murder. And I would like to suggest that this is precisely what

Antigone's argument, her *law*, as she calls it ("Such was the law by which I honored you"), aims at.

This is what makes Polyneices quite exceptional; this is what makes Antigone stand against the will of the city in this case: not the fact that Polyneices is also a human being, like everybody else, but the fact that he is *not* a human being *like everybody else* (and that he is more like the singular other side of every human being, their unhuman side). It is not his virtues, nor simply his general humanity, but his crime and the peculiar nature of his tie to her that make him singular and worth defending, honoring, at the price of her own life (and that of many others). Lacan's reading in the *Ethics* seminar already takes a first step in that direction, although I think that a couple of further steps could and should be taken in order to fully appreciate all the stakes of what takes place in *Antigone* in this regard.

No mediation is possible here except that of this desire with its radically destructive character. The fruit of the incestuous union has split into two brothers, one of whom represents power and the other crime. There is no one to assume the crime and the validity of crime apart from Antigone.

Between the two of them, Antigone chooses to be purely and simply the guardian of the being of the criminal as such. No doubt things could have been resolved if the social body had been willing to pardon, to forget and cover over everything with the same funeral rites. It is because the community refuses this that Antigone is required to sacrifice her own being in order to maintain that essential being which is the family *Ate*, and that is the theme or true axis on which the whole tragedy turns. Antigone perpetuates, eternalizes, immortalizes that *Ate*. (Lacan 1997, 283)

Antigone is the guardian of family *átē*, of its particular misfortune (mischief, ruin, folly)—that is to say, of this singular, unique family *átē*, not of family ties in general.

But then we face the enigma of the *universal* appeal of this drama, and the attempt to define this enigma leads to a different kind of universality. What if this singular family's *átē* is in fact somehow repeated with every family and constitutes the other side of family structure as such (family structure as a symbolic structure caught in the wheels of reproduction, of reproduction by death or loss)? Or, even more generally, of the symbolic order and language as such?

This is another point that Lacan seems to be making in *The Ethics of Psychoanalysis*, relying heavily in his argument on Heidegger and on his notion of the ontological difference. He suggests that the *unique* value involved in Polyneices and his crime is "essentially that of language."

We could sum up his argument as follows. It is only language that operates, that is capable of operating, a radical separation or split between Being as such and all of its historical configurations, peripeties, and characteristics. In this reading, language and its violence are the sole support of what Heidegger called the "ontological difference," the difference between pure Being and *Dasein*, or existence. It is only the violence of language that makes it possible to think, to speak, of pure Being. And Antigone bears witness to this violence and embodies it, because, first, she insists on it in relation to Polyneices: he may be many things—a criminal, a traitor—but he also and simply *is*, and this being is irreducible.

> Antigone's position represents the radical limit that affirms the unique value of his being without reference to any content, to whatever good or evil Polyneices may have done, or to whatever he may be subjected to.
>
> The unique value involved is essentially that of language. Outside of language it is inconceivable, and the being of him who has lived cannot be detached from all he bears with him in the nature of good and evil, of destiny, of consequences for others, or of feelings for himself. That purity, that separation of being from the characteristics of the historical drama he has lived through, is precisely the limit or the *ex nihilo* to which Antigone is attached. It is nothing more than the break that the very presence of language inaugurates in the life of man. (Lacan 1997, 279)

And not only does Antigone insist on this in relation to Polyneices. She also lends her own body to it; she in effect *aestheticizes* it (with some help from Creon) by her own destiny and ordeal: by being walled up alive, situated in that terrifying realm between-two-deaths, by bringing in the perspective of a second death, regarded as the point at which the very cycle of the transformations of nature is annihilated. This situating, this positioning of Antigone, which follows and illuminates the coordinates of her desire, is where the pure and radical signifying separation becomes visible and enters the realm of the aesthetic—hence, again, Antigone's "sublime beauty," or the blinding "splendor of Antigone."

"This is the point where the false metaphors of being (*l'étant*) can be distinguished from the position of Being (*Être*) itself, and we find its place articulated as such, as a limit, throughout the text of *Antigone*" (Lacan 1997, 248). So this is how, in the *Ethics* seminar, Lacan conceives the link between the singular ("unique") and the universal with which *Antigone* presents us. The singular of Polyneices's being or existence, his *criminal* acts, are needed as a "contrast agent" that illuminates the universal, which gets constituted as a horizon (of pure being *qua* being) in a negative way. This reading maps the Heideggerian ontological difference onto the difference that lies at the core of Kantian ethics: the difference between a "pathological" act and a "pure" ethical act. In Kant we have the idea that what characterizes a truly ethical act is that it not only accords with the moral law but also is carried out exclusively because of the moral law, only for the sake of that law, allowing *no other motive* but its unconditional, imperative command, devoid of all particular content. So if I act in perfect accordance with the moral law, yet I do it, for example, because I care about my reputation, or I am scared of God, or I feel pity for the other, this is not acting morally. As a matter of fact, if any kind of *feeling* intervenes (causally) in my act, my act is "pathological" and cannot qualify as a genuine ethical act. And, incidentally, we can see here clearly how this resonates with Antigone and her actions based not on feelings for her brother but on a cold and unconditional "law" she is following.

The problem that arises for Kant, in the configuration of ethics he devises, is that the visibility, discernibility, of moral act is practically null, impossible. How are we to distinguish a true moral act from a false one, if they can look exactly the same and if we have no way of probing other people's hearts and firmly establishing the nonexistence of any, even the noblest, motive? It is at this point that the necessity of the often-problematized link between Kantian ethics and suffering[3] comes into play: an ethical act seems to be able to *appear* only through a sharp contrast constituted by everything that we lose and suffer when we act morally, because this constitutes the only phenomenal measure or proof of the *absence* of any pathological motives and hence of the *presence* of the pure, unconditional law. The latter can be attested to only in a negative way, never directly. And again, in *Antigone* we have both: the ethical dimension of her act is evidenced not only through everything that she is made to suffer because of it (no gain for her in all that) but also by her motives concerning Polyneices as exempt from any "pathological" feelings (that is, from any feelings *tout court*). She acts in this way only because something originating in the pure logic of kinship demands it. The criminal character of Polyneices's existence indicates, by way of contrast, the focal point where it gets disentangled, distinguished, from Being as such—we could add, where it gets disentangled from the Law of Being. To put it simply, were Polyneices not a criminal, this horizon of Being as radically different from everything that a person can be in their existence would remain imperceptible (at least aesthetically, that is, by way of the senses).

The statement "even the worst criminal deserves a burial" acquires a more precise, and interestingly antihumanist, ring here: it serves as the contrast agent that makes us perceive the absolute difference

---

3. See the title of Lacan's seminal essay "Kant with Sade" (Lacan 2006b).

between existence (everything that we are or have been) and the abyss of pure Being, introduced and sustained by the violence of language. Being is not something like the broadest common ground or denominator of all human beings; it is not like a fundamental and shared essence of humanity but pure Difference in respect to everything that constitutes that humanity. In other words, that statement does not say that "all human beings deserve a burial" but, rather, that our right to a burial comes from something that as human beings we *are not*, and have never been, existentially.

However, what gets lost to some extent in this powerful reading, focused as it is on ontological difference, is the *singularity of the singularity* at stake in this particular, "Oedipal" family. Does the phrase "being of the criminal as such" really exhaust this singularity, sum it up? What also gets lost is the argument I developed in chapter 2 on the basis of Lacan's *Seminar XI*, where language appears not only as the support and vehicle of the ontological difference but also as carrying, *smuggling in*, an additional Real at the very level of pure Being or, in Kant's configuration, of pure Law: I attributed it to the undeadness related to the drive, to a singular surplus of life that "represents" death by its own *presence* or occurrence, and not by an absence, not only "in a negative way," as in the case of the Kantian paradigm.

Let me therefore suggest another possible reading, a reading developed not through any kind of extensive exegesis but simply through further insisting on the peculiar and singular point of *Antigone* (and of the whole Theban trilogy), on the singular nature of its singularity: Oedipus is both Antigone's father and her brother. I would claim that this is what is, so to say, "crystallized," condensed, comprised in the figure of the "criminal" Polyneices's rotting body, in his being the last of the brothers, and accounts for the unique, exclusive value that he has for Antigone (and, through her, for all of us). As a way of arguing this, I will now suggest two conclusions, which are certainly related yet also irreducible to each other, constituting what I choose to call Antigone's parallax.

INCEST

The first conclusion would point, from the singularity of the constellation of Antigone, to a singularity, a "pathology," pertaining to
the general structure—in this case, of language. The configuration
we are dealing with in *Antigone* implies and reveals something
more than what is implied in the notion of ontological difference
as entailing the separation of pure Being from any possible content or existential configuration of being. As a matter of fact, it
comes closer to what we could call "another turn of the screw of
ontological difference": something that introduces a strange, unexpected singular content at the very level of pure Being, of Being
as such.[4]

To enable us to understand this idea, it can be illuminating to recall an amusing example of the exact configuration involved in Antigone's relationship to Oedipus (and Polyneices) yet coming from a
very different context. The configuration that interests us here is one
in which a cut, a minus, is represented by something appearing twice,
that is to say, by a *surplus appearance*, a configuration in which
the violence of language involved in our ability to think pure Being,
or simply to speak, is represented not by the abstraction made of any
positive content of being ("even if it is criminal") but by a content
appearing twice, that is to say, by a pathological content or "crime"
adhering to pure Being as such. The fact that Antigone actually has
three brothers and not two finds a rather unexpected echo in a funny
story that Lacan comes up with in *Seminar XI*. He refers to a failure
of—we can imagine—mental health experts, or some other experts,
to recognize a profound logic involved in somebody saying, "I have
three brothers, Paul, Ernest, and me." This person is declared to be,

---

4. The philosophical point following from this would be that "being *qua* being" is necessarily *disoriented* by this singular object, by this additional real. (For more on this notion of
an "object-disoriented ontology," see Zupančič 2017.)

well, a simpleton. But, argues Lacan, "it is quite natural—first the three brothers, Paul, Ernest, and I are counted, and then there is I at the level at which I am to reflect the first I, that is to say, the I who counts" (Lacan 1998, 20). In other words, this seemingly illogical, pathological configuration is exactly how language actually works, how it works all the time. The quote is from the section called "The Unconscious and Repetition"—and, indeed, both repetition and the unconscious are very much what is at issue here.

Could we not say that Antigone, with all her being and her actions, is saying something like, *I have three brothers, Polyneices, Eteocles, and my father?* In other words, is it not salient that the order of brothers is marked for her, in a very concrete and dramatic way, by the irruption, imposition, of an unexpected, "impossible" appearance of the father in the chain of brothers?

This configuration is similar, if not quite identical, to Lacan's example, which can be more neatly related to the way in which language functions generally and at all times, without our noticing it. The logical glitch, the short circuit implied in this configuration, can be recognized in many speech paradoxes, "impossible statements," like the famous liar's paradox. If I say "I'm lying," and I'm really lying, then I'm actually telling the truth; while if I'm telling the truth when I say that I'm lying, then I'm actually lying. Lacan solves this kind of paradox elegantly by distinguishing between the level of enunciation (*énonciation*) and the level of the statement (*énoncé*)— the distinction, precisely, that the example of the three brothers cited earlier is meant to demonstrate. He refuses to gloat over the fascination usually generated by this kind of paradox and "impossible statement." He suggests that one simply needs to distinguish between the "I that counts" and the "I that is counted" and acknowledge the subjective split involved in, and induced by, the fact that we speak at all. Language carries within itself a split that generates a certain type of "impossible" statement or, more precisely, that generates certain statements as logically impossible, although these statements *exist,* are quite common, and are perfectly comprehensible in our everyday use of language.

> It is quite clear that the *I am lying*, despite its paradox, is perfectly valid. Indeed, the *I* of the enunciation is not the same as the *I* of the statement, that is to say, the shifter which, in the statement, designates him. So, from the point at which I state, it is quite possible for me to formulate in a valid way that the *I*—the *I* who, at that moment, formulates the statement—is lying, that he lied a little before, that he is lying afterwards, or even, that in saying *I am lying*, he declares that he has the intention of deceiving. . . .
>
> This division between the statement and the enunciation means that, in effect, from the *I am lying* which is at the level of the chain of the statement—the *am lying* is a signifier, forming part, in the Other, of the treasury of vocabulary in which the *I*, determined retroactively, becomes a signification, engendered at the level of the statement, of what it produces at the level of the enunciation—what results is an *I am deceiving you*. (Lacan 1998, 139)

Lacan further relates this split, which is constitutive of meaning, to the topology of the unconscious, to the so-called primal repression (the Freudian hypothesis of *Urverdrängung*) as structurally preceding all repression proper and making the latter possible. Primal repression would thus coincide with the constitution of the unconscious. I read this as suggesting that the topology and gap of the unconscious is, so to speak, *built into* the structure of language, pertaining to it in an irreducible way. The topology of the unconscious is transmitted to us together with language; it does not occur simply with the first thing we repress but becomes actualized at that precise moment. (This would also imply that what is called the "mastery of language" or "linguistic competence"—being able to talk meaningfully, mistakes notwithstanding—actually coincides with a first actual, and contingent, repression: prior to that we can repeat words, mimic sounds, but not really "speak." Only with our first repression do we appropriate [make part of our subjectivity] the negativity at the core of language, the negativity across which the signifiers run in order to refer to one another and "make sense.") To put it differently, in a way, repression is already at work in speech as such and does not originate simply in subjective psychology. We could also say that this structural "groove" is precisely the point where the general structure or topology of speech and subjective psychology or pathology coincide and turn out to be irreducibly entangled. This further implies that the structure of language is never simply "pure" (nor "purely differential," as structural linguistics maintains), closed upon itself, but carries in itself a germ, a "stain," of its own contingent subjectivation.

This last point is also Lacan's crucial supplement and shift in respect of classical structuralist and poststructuralist theory. Unlike in poststructuralism, in psychoanalysis the subject is not simply an *effect* of the structure (of some fundamentally nonsubjective process); the subject is the lack *in* this structure; the subject is different from subjectivation, from the richness of life-experiences. The subject corresponds to the gap in the symbolic structure, which is precisely why, for Lacan, "subject" is synonymous with "subject of the unconscious"; subject points to the fact that the symbolic, discursive structure is not whole. If symbolic, discursive structures were fully consistent, unproblematic entities, there would be no subject—and several veins of structuralism and poststructuralism posit exactly that: they simply abandon the notion of the subject, instead of recognizing it as a symptomatic point to which one can turn when analyzing and tackling the impasses and contradictions of a given structure. For psychoanalysis, on the other hand, the subject is not simply an effect of the structure but the effect of its inherent contradiction or negativity—which is not the same thing.

Following the example of the statement "I have three brothers, Paul, Ernest, and me" as turning inside out the way in which language functions on an everyday basis, we could in fact venture a rather daring hypothesis about language's intrinsically *incestuous* structure. What is "kinship"? One way of defining it would be to say that it is a delineated symbolic grid (of differences) imprinted on maximal proximity, likeness.

Ferdinand de Saussure famously claimed that in language there are only differences without positive terms and that meaning is produced solely through this differential network. Yet what the Freudian discovery of the unconscious brought to light were precisely "positive entities" in language: what lies at the basis of "unconscious formations," such as puns, slips of the tongue, dreams, is not difference but rather similarity, even "sameness" (of the sound), that is, homophony—a concept that plays a crucial role in what Lacan later termed *lalangue* (Milner 2017; Dolar 2019). To take an example, Freud's patient, in describing her family, says, "they all possess *Geiz* [avarice]—I meant to say *Geist* [spirit]" (Freud 1975, 106). Or there is the following example from the (now almost forgotten) arsenal of "Bushisms": "They misunderestimated me" (Bentonville, Arkansas, November 6, 2000). Here language functions and, paradoxically, also *makes sense* not through purely differential structure but through contamination, contagion, coincidence, short-circuiting, through impossible, "incestuous" liaisons between words or sounds— incestuous because they ignore the law of the difference. So we could say, in language there are only differences, except that there is also incest. This is perhaps how the Freudian contribution to linguistics could be summed up in one sentence.

Let us return to the statement "I have three brothers, Paul, Ernest, and me." Is there not something "incestuous," or akin to it, that strikes us in this statement? Something like an impossible picture of the "I of the count" copulating with the "I who counts," the subject of the statement relating to the subject of enunciation in an impossible, forbidden way? We find it funny and charming when small children speak about themselves in the third person, yet the shift from "Tina wants ice cream" to "I want ice cream" implies a dramatic scene of leaving "Tina" behind, outside, on the side of the others and of things. "Tina" does not disappear from this outside; rather, "Tina" (or any subject of the statement, of the count) disappears from the inside, gets separated from the *I* of enunciation. The shifter *I* does not replace "Tina," fill in the gap of its disappearance on the inside, but rather *marks this gap*, this void. You have to let "Tina" go in order to gain mastery of language, and with it you let go of a certain immediate coincidence with yourself. You can now say "I am Tina," and this simple, basic statement already implies the topology, the gap of the unconscious, its fundamental rift and structure. And while appearing in this way out there, among others, "Tina" also enters into all kinds of objective relations with them and exists objectively, or rather independently, of the *I* that refers to her, conjures up her being on the occasion of speaking.

To relate the split between the *I* of the enunciation and the *I* of the statement to the structure of (the prohibition of) incest may seem more than a little stretched. Incest, we feel, implies something of a substance, usually referred to as "blood"; it also implies, well, a sexual relation. Language, all its juicy paradoxes notwithstanding, constitutes a different kind of order. This is both true and not altogether true. To say "I have three brothers, Paul, Ernest, and me" is obviously not the same as sleeping with Paul or Ernest (or with oneself). But from the perspective of someone like Oedipus, it could very well refer to something in the Real. Could Oedipus not have said, quite realistically, "I have three brothers, Eteocles, Polyneices, and me"? For he is also Jocasta's son, not only her husband, and in his case this statement involves a Real that goes beyond the problem of distinguishing, or blurring the distinction, between the level of enunciation and the level of the statement. In other words, from the perspective of Oedipus, this distinction would seem rather abstract. For in Oedipus's case it gets attached—by being quite literally true—to an additional, surplus Real. This is a fact. Yet it would be wrong to dismiss the difference between enunciation and statement as "abstract" in other cases, where such an additional turn of the screw does not take place. On the contrary, it can be very engaging and consequential, involving all the flesh and blood we want.

As a matter of fact, there is another thread or element of Oedipus's story that bears witness to the difference between enunciation and statement being anything but abstract precisely. This element relates not to his incestuous marriage but to what he does to get himself in the position to marry his mother in the first place.

In other words, it has to do with the famous enigma, the Sphinx's riddle, that lies at the very heart of Oedipus's story and the answer to which opens for him the path to the incestuous throne.

Oedipus's confrontation with the Sphinx redoubles in some ways the function of the oracle to which his parents have responded as they did (by asking the unfortunate herdsman to make him disappear). The Sphinx asks Oedipus what it is that first goes on four feet, then on two, and finally on three. Oedipus replies "man," as a child who crawls, as an adult walking on two feet, and as an old man with a cane. Yet, as Jean-Pierre Vernant has pointed out, the knowledge that enables Oedipus to decipher the riddle of the Sphinx is self-referential; it concerns Oedipus himself. Oedipus's answer is, in a certain sense, "(man)-Oedipus," since Oedipus combines in himself the three generations suggested by the riddle: "By his parricide followed by incest, he installs himself at the place occupied by his father; he confuses in Jocasta his mother and his bride; he identifies himself at the same time with Laius (as Jocasta's husband) and with his children (for whom he is both father and brother), thus mingling together the three generations of the lineage" (Vernant 1972, 127). When Oedipus gives his answer to the riddle, the Sphinx disappears, and the path opens for him to become king of Thebes and marry his mother. Lacan returns to this part of *Oedipus the King* in *Séminaire XVII (The Other Side of Psychoanalysis)*, anticipating Vernant's point. He takes it up in the context of a discussion of the status of knowledge and its relation to truth. What is *truth as knowledge*? Moreover, how can we know without knowledge (or without knowing it)—referring, of course, to the unconscious knowledge? The answer, he suggests, lies in the configuration of the riddle or enigma. Truth as knowledge is structured like a riddle, comparable to the one posed by the Sphinx to Oedipus. Truth as knowledge is a "half-said" (a *mi-dire*), just as the Sphinx is a "half-body," ready to disappear as soon as her riddle is solved. The Sphinx poses a riddle to Oedipus, who answers in a particular way—Lacan emphasizes that many other answers to the riddle of the Sphinx are also possible—and it *is through this answer that he becomes Oedipus.* And Lacan places at the core of this riddle business nothing other than the difference between enunciation and statement:

> If I insisted at length on the difference in level between the utterance [*énonciation*] and the statement [*énoncé*], it was so that the function of the enigma would make sense. An enigma is most likely that, an utterance. I charge you with the task of making it into a statement. Sort that out as best you can—as Oedipus did—and you will bear the consequences. That is what is at issue in an enigma. (2007, 36–37)

We can see how the distinction between the level of enunciation (here translated as "utterance") and the level of the statement is deployed here as a possible way in which the subject becomes very concretely involved in the symbolic order that determines them. By making statements out of enunciations, we stake something of ourselves in this "game," which has material, concrete consequences.

Knowledge as truth is structured as a riddle—but it is not the kind of riddle whose answer we can find written at the bottom of the page or in a dictionary of riddles. The subject who solves riddles with the help of a dictionary of riddles knows, in fact, many things, but this knowledge has nothing to do with truth. For in order for the effect of truth to occur, the subject must throw in their word like a wager, as Oedipus did—which makes him different from his "typical" mythical counterparts whom the gods assist by whispering the right answer in their ears. As Jean-Joseph Goux has pointed out, one of several atypical features of Oedipus's myth is that he vanquishes the Sphinx without the assistance of the gods and without even the assistance of mortals, like the counsel of a wise man or a prophet (1990, 24).

It is this knowledge, the knowledge that might be called the knowledge guaranteed by the big Other, that Oedipus lacks or steps out of. No one, neither a divinity nor some wise man, can reassure him in advance that his answer will be right (or "true"). And in spite of this, he ventures his answer. In so doing, he comes closer than his mythical counterparts to the dimension of the act in the proper sense of the term.

But what does this mean? Does it imply that Oedipus's act is an act of "transgression" and betrayal of the Other or of the tradition, as Goux suggests, seeing his answer to the Sphinx as itself constituting the original crime (of "philosophical arrogance"),[5] in relation to which his parricide and incest are nothing but consequences—punishment for this original crime? Moreover, if there are several possible answers to the Sphinx's question (as Lacan claims),[6] does this not imply that truth is wholly arbitrary? Could Oedipus, who does not have his dictionary of riddles at hand, then have given any answer whatever? Does not such a relativistic view obscure rather than clarify the function of truth? Does it not lead to the conclusion that at the end of the day, truth does not exist, because there is no "objective" criterion of truth?

The answer to all of these questions is no, and it is precisely this that we learn in the tragic story of Oedipus. Lacan's two faces of knowledge can be summarized as follows:

1. Knowledge as the "knowledge that knows itself" is the knowledge behind a statement supported by an anticipated guarantee (at the level of enunciation), in the sense that the Other is always-already there, ready to offer a guarantee for the statement the subject makes out of this enunciation (or "utterance").

2. Knowledge as truth is a word, a statement for which the subject alone holds the guarantee in an act of anticipation, of "precipitate identification."

---

5. The title of Goux's book is *Œdipe philosophe*, "Oedipus the Philosopher."
6. And the Chimera put an enigma to Oedipus the man who perhaps already had a complex, but certainly not the one he gave his name to. He replied in a particular way, and that was how he became Oedipus.

> There could have been many other replies to what the Chimera asked him. For example, he might have said, "Two feet, three feet, four feet—that's Lacan's schema." That would have produced quite a different result. He could also have said, "It's a man, a man as a baby. As a baby he starts out on four feet. He walks on two, he acquires a third, and instantly he flies as straight as an arrow into his mother's stomach." That is, in effect, what one calls, rightly, the Oedipus complex. (Lacan 2007, 36)

This powerful definition of knowledge as truth does not yet answer questions linked to the absence of "objective" criteria of truth and to the "relativism" of truth. Let us therefore make it more precise. It is quite true that, in a certain sense and faced with this kind of enigma, the subject can give "any answer whatever" and that prior to this answer, there is no statement that could be established in advance as "true." Nevertheless, when the subject gives their answer, they *actually give* something—they must give or offer their word and thus can be *taken at their word*. The moment the subject gives their answer to the riddle, the words of their response are neither true nor false; they are an anticipation of the truth that becomes truth only as consequence of these words. This is also Lacan's point when he claims that the structure of (psychoanalytic) interpretation is of exactly the same nature, which is why it concerns "knowledge as truth":

> If the analytic experience finds itself in the position where it owes some
> of its nobility to the Oedipal myth, it is because it preserves the sharp
> edge of the enunciation of the oracle. And I will say even more: that
> interpretation in the analysis remains at the same level, it only becomes
> true in its consequences, precisely as it is the case with the oracle.
> (Lacan 2006a, 13)

The function of the riddle in *Oedipus the King* thus redoubles the function of the oracle, since—as we have already seen—the riddle can be read as asking who unites within himself three generations. Oedipus answers with a single word, and he becomes the hostage of this word, the truth of which he will live and attest to at a very heavy price. The way in which Lacan relates this peculiar structure of the enigma to the more general structure of the difference between enunciation ("utterance") and statement indicates forcefully how this general, principal or "abstract" difference can be—and often is—involved very directly in a concrete subjective destiny.

Relating in this way the difference between the enunciation and the statement to the structure of enigma, and to the concrete

consequences and stakes that the answer to it can have for our subjective destiny, should therefore preclude conceiving the difference
at stake as a purely linguistic abstraction. For it is not, and it affects
all speaking beings in different, often dramatic ways: it is very much
involved in creating, driving, and forming the life that "carries" it.
Yet—to return to the starting point of this discussion—the *incest*
part nevertheless appears to pertain to Oedipus's singularity, to
the particular, specific statement that *he* makes on the basis of the
Sphinx's enigmatic enunciation, not to this structural difference in
general. *He* brings in the incest. Yes. But if we are still tempted to
suggest that there exists something like an incestuous dimension of
language as such, of which Oedipus is the emblem and that constitutes the other side of the universal prohibition of incest, the reasons are as follows.

Let us look at this for a moment from another perspective: from
the perspective of the incest itself. What does incest entail, exactly?
Cultural anthropology shows that although its prohibition appears
to be universal (we find incest taboos in all cultures), what any
given culture defines as incest is also quite "arbitrary," or simply very
different. (In some cultures, for example, sexual relations between
brothers and sisters are even encouraged.) According to Claude Lévi-
Strauss (1969), the only universal rule is that *some* relations are prohibited; this led him to posit that the incest taboo is the general
condition of the very passage or leap from nature to culture, regardless of what exactly is prohibited in this or that culture.

I would claim, however, that the difficulty is even more specific.
For even if we focus on one particular culture and its definition of
incest, it is still hard to say what exactly incest refers to. It never refers simply to (our relationship with) another *person*, defined by a
specific place in the symbolic structure (mother, father, brother, sister,
etc.), that is to say, defined by their symbolic function. It also and
simultaneously refers to something particular *in* this person (something particular in the particular), usually referred to as "blood." This
reference to "blood" in the prohibition of incest should not be taken

too anecdotally. It is most interesting and also interestingly different from, for example, what is known as *Blut und Boden* types of ideas and ideologies. We could say that in the case of incest, the "sameness" of blood refers to a surplus sameness that cannot be simply integrated into the symbolic relationship of kinship, fully assimilated in and reduced to it. "Blood" (the image, the idea of blood) actually seems to be related precisely to that undead surplus that—in the case of Oedipus—persists even when symbolic ties are cut: it is because of the "blood" relation, not because of the symbolic relation, that Oedipus could be, and in fact was, accused of parricide and incest.

Yet, does blood in this case refer simply to something physical? No; it is more like a physical manifestation or image of the *Real* of a symbolic relationship (of kinship). We seem to be going around in circles here. These days we speak of "shared genetic material" instead of "blood," and we objectify this surplus Real. But what degree of shared genetic material qualifies as incest? More than by objective (genetic) criteria, this is defined by symbolic criteria. For example, a stepfather's relation with his stepdaughter would still be (rightly) considered as "incestuous," even if technically it is not. In other words, "incest" seems to be more than what is implied in its strict technical definition. Perhaps we could even say that incest is precisely that which is more than its technical definition. Whether we approach it from the symbolic side or from the empirical (physical) side, it always seems to be in the "more" that eludes them. It is more than a symbolic relation (hence the reference to blood or to genes), yet it is also more than blood or genes; there is always a surplus of signification attached to it.

In this sense, and from this perspective, could we not say that "incest" is precisely the impossible coincidence of the two, the impossible point where one slips into the other, "nature" into "culture" and "culture" into "nature"? The prohibition of incest is neither cultural nor natural, but at the same time it is both. Incest is that something in nature more than nature, and it is that something in culture more than culture. So, again, what exactly is incest?

In chapter 2, I dwelt at some length at Lacan's rather daring and extraordinary proposal that the signifier came into the world through sexual reality and sexual division because of the latter's involvement in reproduction, reproduction involving death (a minus) as its internal moment. Could we not say that "incest" is precisely what names the impossible point of this conjunction of sexual reality (including the genetic, chromosome combinatory involved in reproduction) and the signifier (purely symbolic relationship)? It is neither here nor there, yet it is both. Is incest not the name of the impossible, inconceivable *missing link* between nature and culture? However, Lévi-Strauss's claim that incest taboos marked humanity's transition from "nature" to "culture" acquires a different emphasis here. For Lévi-Strauss, this prohibition is the ground; it is conceived as the necessary condition of exchange (of women as gifts in a reciprocal networking of the social). It forces members of a group to go outside the group. In this sense, incest taboo, so to say, "explains" the passage from nature to culture. What I am suggesting here is different; it concerns the way in which the impossible, nonexisting passage or junction of nature and culture (symbolic relations)—precisely *as impossible*—"explains" the incest taboo, its function. The incest taboo is there to cover up, with its prohibition, the impossibility of this passage or conjunction; it is the paramount case of prohibiting the impossible, of prohibiting what is in itself impossible—a fundamental operation that renders the impossible symbolically manageable, approachable. Symbolic prohibition covers a real impossibility and invites transgression. Transgression presents the ontological impossibility as something that is, in principle, possible yet unattainable, lingering out there, beyond the limits imposed by the law.

This brings us back to the discussion of "unwritten laws" in chapter 1. Could we not say that the incest taboo covers, protects, the leaking structure of culture, of the symbolic order as such? That it staunches the leak in the culture, the point where the latter is not fully constituted or operative? As the missing link between nature and culture, incest itself is something like an enigma or a Sphinx, a half-body, half-signifier. It suggests the image of "nature" copulating with "culture," producing monstrous, *strange* creatures that ancient mythology is rather full of. It constitutes the irreducible, persisting obverse side of "proper" human beings. The important—indeed, central—role of the famous "Ode to Man" in *Antigone* can be directly related to this interrogation of "the other side of man," this strangest of creatures, of wonders. Reread from this perspective, the first strophe of the poem does indeed suggest a bizarre scene of a rather violent "copulation" between culture and nature, between man and the Earth:

> Many the wonders but nothing is stranger than man.
> This thing crosses the sea in the winter's storm,
> making his path through the roaring waves.
> And she, the greatest of gods, the Earth—
> ageless she is, and unwearied—he wears her away
> as the ploughs go up and down from year to year
> and his mules turn up the soil. (*Antigone*, 334–341)

The image is striking and resonates with several things discussed in this book. Just as we saw this scenario play out in the case of sexual reproduction, the "ageless," immortal Nature (Earth) now gets dragged into temporality, exhaustion, and death; it gets pulled into (human) temporality, which has death as its intrinsic condition, as well as the condition of its own, specific immortality. That is why death remains the only thing that man, with all his power and abilities, "cannot find an escape from" (*Antigone*, 359–360).

Many things have been written, from the feminist perspective, about how femininity is persistently associated with nature, and masculinity with culture. And that trope is indeed there, in the preceding verses. Yet from the perspective we are developing here, we could ask: Is not this persistent image of womanhood as representing nature in *human* relationships precisely a way of covering up the impossible, unspeakable Thing at the core of both nature and culture, their "missing link," which, if it existed, could only be monstrous and

undead? In other words, what is at stake is not only a "naturaliza-
tion" of femininity but also a feminization/humanization of "nature,"
presenting it as something always-already meant to be copulating
with culture, "complementing it," as women are supposed to do with
men. Positing the terms of sexual difference as aligned with the na-
ture/culture divide casts this divide itself as something "natural" and
unproblematic (which it is precisely not)—as long as women "know
their place." And there is an important discussion of this last point
in *Antigone* (in her dialog with Ismene), to which I will return in the
next section. Sexual difference becomes "essentialized" in this way
so as to avoid or cover up the irreducible gap between nature and
culture, the radical "loss of nature" implied by the symbolic and its
functioning. "Women" are charged with the task of representing nature *within* culture: an infinite task, never quite coinciding with what
was originally lost. What I see as the Lacanian revolution in this context is to envisage sexual difference not as a difference *between*
sexes or sexual identities but as a cut, a negativity, a loss, induced by
speech. This cut, this negativity, is a "problem" that the sexes have
in common and to which they respond by different ways of symbol-
izing it. Contrary to this perspective, "essentialization" consists in
extracting this shared negativity or loss and transposing it into a
divide *between* the sexes as positive entities or essences. At the same
time—and this is pertinent to this discussion—it amounts to covering up the missing link between nature and culture. Or perhaps we
could put this the other way around: it covers, veils, the link that exists and persists in the form of their monstrous copulation, which is
neither natural nor cultural. We could also relate this idea to the discussion of the link between sexuality (sexual reproduction) and
symbolic order (language) in chapter 2: something is "lost" in reproductive sexuality as dependent on individual death; and the relation
to the Other is not simply the relation to the other sex but the
relation between the living subject and that which they lose by having to go, for reproduction, through the sexual cycle.

What the idea of "incest" suggests in this respect is a sexuality, sexual reproduction, without division and death, because it escapes temporality, successions of generations perpetuating the species, the gap between the individual and the species. But precisely in this sense, incest is itself a mythical Thing; it does not exist. More precisely, it exists only as taboo, *as prohibition* of incest: a prohibition of something that is in itself impossible. Empirical incest, which of course exists, is something else; it involves both desire and death. It would be wrong to see an empirical incestuous relationship as some kind of plunging into eternity, into a fullness of enjoyment, without loss. Rather, empirical incest is the paradoxical (and hence) "monstrous" figure in which the condition of desire (lack) directly appears as the Other. The Other is not the carrier of the mysterious object, implying an objectification of the Other (the Other appearing as object of desire); what occurs is, rather, an "otherization" of the object, the object (lack, death) appearing as Other. It is not simply a return to some primordial oneness or fullness; it involves desire, and hence lack, yet with an "impossible" twist in which the Other embodies, so to say, their own disappearance, loss, death. It is like desire turning on itself, desiring its own condition as its object.

It is also in this sense that *Antigone* is a drama of desire.

DESIRE

Let us return to the starting point of these two concluding parallax variations: Oedipus happens to be both Antigone's father and her brother, which is precisely what gets "crystallized," comprised, in Polyneices and his crime, in the unique value he has for Antigone as the last of the brothers. With all her being and actions, I suggested, Antigone is saying something like, "I have three brothers, Polyneices, Eteocles, and Oedipus." The consequence of this is that the name for Polyneices's surplus, unique value is actually "Oedipus," yet Oedipus not simply as father and not simply as brother but as that short circuit between the two that contaminates the "ontological difference" introduced by the signifier with a scandalous *indiffer-ence*, indistinction, and ties, tightens, the loop of the biological and of the symbolic (kinship) in their very heterogeneity.

The key to this short circuit is of course Jocasta, the mother of all five (Oedipus, Antigone, Ismene, Polyneices, and Eteocles) and at the same time Oedipus's wife. It is with this "key" in mind that we can introduce the question of Antigone's desire and further unfold a par-ticular aspect of Lacan's reading of Antigone as the figure of desire that is often forgotten; it is forgotten because his reading involves two components, only one of which usually gets all the attention.

To understand, as Lacan does, Antigone's claim, her inflexible in-sistence, her actions, her sacrifice as an issue of desire (of "pure desire") is not something that imposes itself as obvious; it is not some-thing that the reading of Sophocles's play would immediately suggest. It becomes "obvious" only from the perspective in which desire is conceived in psychoanalysis: that is to say, as fundamentally related to the modality of the *question mark*, of questioning, addressed to the Other: *What am I to you? What do you want? (You are demand-ing this and that, but what is it that you actually want, or aim at?).* Desire is essentially related to an interrogation of the Other and of one's place in relationship to the Other—and to what remains unan-swered in every answer. Antigone embodies this in two different ways. If desire is emphatically not the same thing as various "wishes," this is because desire emerges through the difference to these wishes and demands: *You wish, you demand this and that, but what do you actually want?* Antigone emerges as a figure of pure desire pre-cisely because, with her words and actions, she *incites in others* this tenacious question: *What does she want?* She states what she wants from the outset, yet there is no one in the play who is not baffled at one point or another by this question: Okay, she wants to bury Poly-neices, but what does she *actually* want? It starts with Ismene, in her opening dialog with Antigone, and it reemerges again and again. It seems particularly pressing because Antigone appears to know quite well that her persistence will not succeed in accomplishing what she demands (to get Polyneices buried). So why does she do it? What does she want? Is this just an empty stubbornness? What is she truly aiming at?

So on the one hand we have Antigone's desire and its enigma. In this respect, Antigone seems to be at the opposite pole from Oedipus. She is like the Sphinx: her demand, although clear, remains deeply enigmatic and functions precisely like an enunciation, which those who are confronted with it will have to make into a statement and bear the consequences, which they will indeed end up doing.[7] There will be consequences for everybody. Unlike Oedipus, Antigone is not the hostage of her word. Rather, she is a hostage of desire, of the way in which her desire relates to the desire of the Other.

This point constitutes the other emphasis of Lacan's reading, which is often lost in translation. As I have already pointed out, the pivotal point of the drama of desire that reaches its peak in *Antigone* is in fact Jocasta, Antigone's mother. It is worth recalling that in Lacan's reading of *Hamlet* in *Seminar VI* (2019), when discussing the classic psychoanalytic suggestion of Hamlet's Oedipal desire, he makes a surprising move that turns many things upside down. According to the classic psychoanalytic narrative, Hamlet's problem is that Claudius carries out Hamlet's own repressed Oedipal desire: he kills his father and sleeps with his mother. Guilty because his unconscious desire has thus found an unexpected realization, Hamlet is paralyzed, unable to act against Claudius. Lacan shatters this classic narrative by pointing out something that is in fact quite obvious if you think about it: the central problem and question for Hamlet is not *his* desire (the supposedly secret, unconscious desire for his mother); the vexing question and problem for Hamlet is his *mother's desire*. This is what haunts and unsettles him; here lies the unbearable scandal of his mother's relationship with Claudius, which constitutes the core of

---

7. Interestingly, when talking about the Sphinx in its relationship to Oedipus, Lacan suggests that it incarnates "the original characteristic of the hysteric's discourse" (2007, 36).

the so-called closet scene: How can she be with this man? How can she want him, desire him, sleep with him? How can she have a desire at all, now that her husband, Hamlet's father, is dead? What does she want? Where does her desire put him, Hamlet?[8]

Lacan's point is thus rather surprising: the problem of "Oedipal" desire is not the son's desire for his mother but the fact and the enigma of the mother's desire itself and the effect of this enigma on posterity. Lacan repeats and enhances this point concerning "Oedipal desire" in relation to Oedipus himself yet—and this in itself is most interesting and telling—in the context of *Antigone* and concerning the heroine of the play, not concerning Oedipus, who, after all, gave his name to the (in)famous complex. Yet this is not so surprising if we bear in mind that Oedipus actually gets cheated out of his "Oedipal desire" by the protective machinations of his parents, which put him in the position of realizing this desire without ever being able to develop it, to properly own it. But it becomes an issue in *Antigone* and for Antigone, who indeed takes the stage as a kind of anti-Hamlet: anti-Hamlet in the sense that, unlike Hamlet, she demands the recognition, remembrance, honoring of the mother's criminal desire. Here is Lacan on this subject:

> Think about it. What happens to her desire? Shouldn't it be the desire of the Other and be linked to the desire of the mother? The text alludes to the fact that the desire of the mother is the origin of everything. The desire of the mother is the founding desire of the whole structure, the one that brought into the world the unique offspring that are Eteocles,

---

8. To quote just the opening of that long and powerful scene (in the midst of which Hamlet manages to kill Polonius, as if it were nothing):

QUEEN GERTRUDE:
Have you forgot me?

HAMLET:
No, by the rood, not so:
You are the queen, your husband's brother's wife;
And—would it were not so—you are my mother.

Polyneices, Antigone and Ismene; but it is also a criminal desire. Thus at the origin of tragedy and of humanism we find once again an impasse that is the same as Hamlet's, except strangely enough it is even more radical.

No mediation is possible here except that of this desire [Antigone's] with its radically destructive character. The fruit of the incestuous union has split into two brothers, one of whom represents power and the other crime. There is no one to assume the crime and the validity of crime apart from Antigone. Between the two of them, Antigone chooses to be purely and simply the guardian of the being of the criminal as such. (1997, 282–283)

To the "impasse" similar to that of Hamlet, Antigone thus reacts very differently. What prevails is the enigma of desire in its disturbing, irreducible facticity and its weight for a subjective destiny.

To say that Oedipal tragedy plays out around the question of maternal desire as the "impossible," "criminal," and enigmatic desire of the Other thus involves a radical double conceptual refocusing of what is at stake in desire. The well-known Lacanian claim that "desire of the subject is always desire of the Other" does not, of course, mean that the subject simply desires the same thing as the other (copying the other's desire, so to speak). It means above all that the subject's desire originates in the enigma and interrogation of the desire of the Other; that is to say, it originates in *that which eludes the Other as well*, in the irreducible contingency of desire. There is something in the Other that the Other is not the master or mistress of. *Why* does the Other want what they want? This is the question and the emphasis that bind the subject's desire to the desire of the Other. "Fidelity to desire" is in this sense fidelity to its question, fidelity to the fact that desire *is* a question: *the* question, even.

But in the case of Antigone, the desire of the Other is not only a question, an enigma, a source of uncertainty; for Antigone, the desire of the Other is, so to speak, a most basic existential fact that affects her—and the whole of Oedipus's family—quite considerably more dramatically than other mortals. It is on behalf of that desire that she can say the "impossible": "I have three brothers, Polyneices, Eteocles, and my father."

Polyneices, to whom Creon refuses assimilation into the symbolic order, remains as the last existing, albeit rotting, embodiment of this paradoxical desire (not counting Ismene).[9] And this is why, in his— and only his—case, Antigone is willing to persist to the end or, rather, *beyond the end*—quite literally from the grave.

What would it mean, therefore, from this perspective, to characterize Antigone's desire as "pure desire"? At first sight, it would seem that Antigone's desire is "pure" since, beyond or below all possible metonymical objects, it aims at the Other's desire as such, at the fact that the Other is not only there but desires. The desire of the Other indicates that there is a point where the Other, so to speak, falls out of its own structure, does not cover it entirely; it shows—to use the usual wording—that the Other itself is "lacking." But this lack in the Other is not the whole story; the lack itself has its obverse "positive" side: it functions as the entry point of contingency, and it has the power to transform what takes place at the level of this contingency into subjective necessity or destiny. "Pure desire" in this sense is not something abstract or purified of all particular objects; it affirms itself only with a particular or, rather, with a singular object. Here again Antigone's "explanation" of her actions, her insistence that she would do it only for this particular brother and no one else, is highly significant and must not be forgotten. Purity of desire is not contradicted by the existence of a singular object through which it affirms itself. Moreover, our "destiny" (in its very inevitability or necessity) is precisely how we are determined by a contingency as the entry point of desire. Antigone clearly feels compelled by this contingency—the contingency testifying to the fact that desire, in spite its "structural" nature, is not just a matter of structure but also of (good or bad) *luck*, of an "improbable cause." The word "fortune" perfectly unites both

9. Because Ismene is a woman, because she is not a "criminal," or because she discounts herself from the very start, as we shall see in a moment?

dimensions, that of a necessary fate and of contingent luck. In this respect, a "pure desire" could also be described as the subject's clinging on to pure contingency. In other words, desire is the mark and the carrier of a contingency, which in the long run appears to be more imperative and necessary than any structural or objective necessity. It is only through contingency that the truly compelling Necessity emerges and binds the subject. Or not.

Antigone begins with the dialog between the two sisters, the only surviving descendants of the "criminal" desire of the Other. Antigone immediately suggests what seems absolutely obvious to her: that in the face of Creon's decree, the sisters can do only one thing: combine their forces and bury Polyneices, even though being stoned to death is the announced punishment for this deed. Ismene sees things differently: in a sense, she is right, but precisely for the same reason, she is also wrong. She thinks that by doing as Antigone suggests they would achieve nothing but add their own disgrace and shame to the already existing disgrace and shame of the whole family. And she argues that this is all the more pointless because they are women.

Remember, sister, how our father
perished abhorred, ill-famed:
himself with his own hand, through his own curse
destroyed both eyes.
Remember next his mother and his wife
finishing life in the shame of the twisted noose.
And third, two brothers on a single day,
poor creatures, murdering, a common doom
each with his arm accomplished on the other.
And now look at the two of us alone.
We'll perish terribly if we violate law
and try to cross the royal vote and power.
We must remember that we two are women,
So not to fight with men;
and that since we are subject to stronger power
we must hear these orders, or any that may be worse. (*Antigone*, 49–64)

Antigone responds to this with cold contempt. "Be what you want to," she retorts (71), refusing to be "a woman" as described by Ismene. Yet I would add that far from abolishing sexual difference by saying this, she actually makes it appear precisely as pure yet irreducible difference: not a difference between two elements that could be described in this or that way but *a difference that makes a difference*, a difference that exposes rather than conceals the negativity intrinsic to the symbolic order as such.

And clearly Antigone does not think that by going along with Creon's decree they could in any way avoid their already shameful, "ill-famed" destiny. They are already part of it. The only thing they can do is to subjectively choose, affirm, this destiny and shame. This is the only freedom at their disposal: the difference they can make. Yet—and this is a big "yet"—freely choosing this necessity is not an empty gesture of acceptance but can take place only as *an act of desire*; it is by no means the same as a resigned acceptance of one's fate. Neither is it about making oneself believe that one "in fact" desires what is inevitable anyway; it is not about presenting necessity as one's own choice. No, something else is at stake here: the violent, splitting *emergence* of desire affirms or, rather, *(re)establishes* the ultimately contingent nature of necessity, in this case of the family's *átē*. Not as a means of relativizing it, but as a means of interposing between the necessity and contingency the dimension of *truth* as that which becomes true only in its consequences.

This could be seen as another, liberating or emancipatory effect of sublimation and as an interesting way of understanding Lacan's suggestion that "no mediation is possible here except that of this desire with its radically destructive character." Mediation in what sense, with respect to what? With respect to the opacity of the incest and of incestuous desire, of different generations "falling/collapsing into one," mediation with respect to the "father" falling into the "brother"—or, to risk a more general hypothesis, with respect to the incestuous other side of language and of the symbolic order appearing *within* this symbolic order itself, as it does in the configuration at issue in the three Theban plays. It is with the sheer force of Antigone's desire—or, rather, with desire as her only force—that she keeps the two levels at play separate. Desire is literally the only ground she stands on, the only ground she *can* stand on.

I started this book by pointing out that *Antigone* comes into focus (of rewriting and interpretation) every time there is some significant tectonic shift or crisis in the social fabric, in the symbolic structuring of the law, or in the wider realm of morality or *Sittlichkeit*. This is because Antigone's singular fate embodies a structural impasse in the symbolic order—the impasse that comes to light particularly at moments of crisis and requires a restructuring of the symbolic order. More precisely, Antigone does not embody this structural impasse but, rather, *the excess* that it inevitably produces. She is a subjective figure of this excess that shatters its ruthless objective accumulation. What does this mean, particularly in our modern context? We have become accustomed to the pressure of objective excess, to the accumulation of the surplus that defines our social order as its required component, that is to say, as (surplus) *value*. At the same time, we have also become accustomed to condemning any subjective surplus—that is to say, any surplus of subjectivity—as harmfully excessive and disturbingly *hysterical*. This condemnation does not in any way contradict the ideological valuing of individual lives and choices, of personal peculiarities, of our "precious uniqueness." On the contrary, it goes hand in hand with it, transposing every problem into our personal problem, to be dealt with by personal growth or treatment. Egocentrism is not a land of subjective singularities, it is rather like a factory, an assembly line of individualities, all similar, if not all the same, adhering to a set of predetermined choices that exclude many others as utterly unthinkable, impossible. The abundance of different choices obfuscates their inexorable uniformity when it comes to the exclusion of any difference that would indeed make a difference.

Subjectivity is something other than this neoliberal valorization of individualities; it is "hysterical" in its essence. It aims not at uniqueness, or at its personal rights, but at what is rotten in the state of things, in the order of things. Freud saw this very clearly. Hysteria is never just a personal problem: it is a problem of a *certain structuring* of power and of social links. And although it is true that the hysteric is usually part of the configuration she denounces, it is also true that hers is *the* subjective position that makes this problem perceptible and impossible to ignore. In this precise sense, the problem of the hysteric is almost always our problem too, whether we care to hear about it or not—not simply because she makes it our problem but because the problem actually exists independently of her, "objectively." Hysteria is a subjectivation of that problem, not simply a "subjective problem."

Antigone stands at the extreme point of this subjectivation. This, I believe, explains the "destructive" nature of her desire. In a sense, it is precisely because she puts an end to all future that Antigone belongs to the future. She is a figure of alternative future(s). I think Žižek made this point forcefully in his version of *Antigone* by not simply siding with the heroine but transposing the play so that it gets three different endings or, as we might put it, three different futures: (1) Creon prevails, as in the original; (2) Antigone prevails; and (3) the Chorus intervenes in their dispute and takes over. I would simply add that the third, collective ending—or future—also emerges as a possibility *because* of Antigone and her "hysterical" subjectivation, the subjectivation that turns the rotting body of Polyneices into a showcase for what is rotten in the *state* of Thebes.

WORKS CITED

Baas, Bernard. (1992). *Le désir pur*. Louvain: Peeters.

Blumenberg, Hans. (1985). *The Legitimacy of the Modern Age*. Cambridge, Mass.: MIT Press.

Butler, Judith. (2000). *Antigone's Claim: Kinship between Life and Death*. New York: Columbia University Press.

Copjec, Joan. (2002). *Imagine There Is No Woman: Ethics and Sublimation*. Cambridge, Mass.: MIT Press.

Dolar, Mladen. (2009). "Freud and the Political." *Theory & Event* vol. 12, issue 3, https://philpapers.org/rec/DOLFAT.

Dolar, Mladen. (2019). "Sophist's Choice." *Crisis & Critique* vol. 6, issue 1, 67–84.

Freud, Sigmund. (1975). *The Psychopathology of Everyday Life*. London: Penguin.

Freud, Sigmund. (2001). "Instincts and Their Vicissitudes." *The Standard Edition of the Complete Psychological Works of Sigmund Freud*. Vol. 14. London: Vintage Books.

Goux, Jean-Joseph. (1990). *Œdipe philosophe*. Paris: Aubier.

Hertmans, Stefan. (2017). *Antigone in Molenbeek*. Amsterdam: De Bezige Bij.

Kantorowicz, Ernst. (2016). *The King's Two Bodies: A Study in Medieval Political Theology*. Princeton, N.J.: Princeton University Press.

Lacan, Jacques. (1997). *The Ethics of Psychoanalysis*. New York: Norton.

Lacan, Jacques. (1998). *The Four Fundamental Concepts of Psychoanalysis*. New York: Norton.

Lacan, Jacques. (2006a). *Le séminaire, livre XVIII. D'un discours qui ne serait pas du semblant*. Paris: Seuil.

Lacan, Jacques. (2006b). "Kant with Sade." In *Écrits*. Trans. Bruce Fink, 645–668. New York: Norton.

Lacan, Jacques. (2007). *The Other Side of Psychoanalysis*. New York: Norton.

Lacan, Jacques. (2011). *Le séminaire, livre XIX. . . . ou pire*. Paris: Seuil.

Lacan, Jacques. (2019). *Desire and Its Interpretation*. Cambridge, Mass.: Polity.

Lefort, Claude. (1988). "The Death of Immortality?" In *Democracy and Political Theory*, 256–282. Minneapolis: University of Minnesota Press.

Lévi-Strauss, Claude. (1969). *The Elementary Structures of Kinship*. Boston: Beacon.

Milner, Jean-Claude. (2017). "Back and Forth from Letter to Homophony." *Problemi International* vol. 1, issue 1, 81–98.

Sade, Marquis de. (1994). *Juliette*. New York: Grove. Kindle edition.

Santner, Eric. (2011). *The Royal Remains: The People's Two Bodies and the Endgames of Sovereignty*. Chicago: University of Chicago Press.

Shamsie, Kamila. (2017). *Home Fire*. London: Bloomsbury.

Sophocles. (1982). *The Three Theban Plays: Antigone, Oedipus the King, Oedipus at Colonus*. Trans. Robert Fagles. New York: Penguin Books.

Sophocles. (2013). *Sophocles I: Antigone, Oedipus the King, Oedipus at Colonus*. Trans. Elisabeth Wyckoff, David Grene, and Robert Fitzgerald. Chicago: University of Chicago Press.

Vernant, Jean-Pierre. (1972). "Ambiguïté et renversement. Sur la structure énigmatique d'Œdipe roi." In *Mythe et tragédie en Grèce ancienne*, 101–131. Paris: Libraire François Maspero.

Žižek, Slavoj. (1992). *Looking Awry. An Introduction to Jacques Lacan through Popular Culture*. Cambridge, Mass.: MIT Press.

Žižek, Slavoj. (1999). *The Ticklish Subject*. London: Verso.

Žižek, Slavoj. (2008). *Violence*. London: Picador.

Žižek, Slavoj. (2016). *Antigone*. London: Bloomsbury Academic.

Zupančič, Alenka. (2017). *What Is Sex?* Cambridge, Mass.: MIT Press.

INDEX

Aeschylus, 22
aestheticization, 55
Anouilh, Jean, 5–6
antagonism, 2–3
Antigone (adaptation) (Anouilh), 5–6
Antigone (adaptation) (Žižek), 1, 82
Antigone (film) (Deraspe), 1
Antigone (Sophocles): adaptations of, 1–2,
5–6, 10, 17, 18–19, 82; background
story of, 5–6; death and funeral rites
in (*see* death; funeral rites; undeadness);
family in (*see* family); incest and desire
in (*see* desire; incest; sexual reproduction and sexuality); original drama, 1,
2–7; parallax view of, 3–4, 57, 73; in
Theban Trilogy, 4–5; violence and
unwritten laws in (*see* unwritten laws;
violence)
"Antigone" (adaptation) (Schlöndorff), 19
Antigone in Molenbeek (Hertman), 1, 19
Assange, Julian, 17, 20

Baas, Bernard, 45
Being vs. existence, 54–57, 58
Blumenberg, Hans, 47
burial rites. *See* funeral rites

cannibal joke, 6, 11–13, 17
Chorus, 1, 41–42, 82
Claudius (character), 75–76
coldness, 2, 52, 56
consequences, embodiment of, 16–17

Copjec, Joan, 46–47, 48–49
Creon (character): conflict and confrontation
with, 3, 4, 23; desire to counter decree
of, 79–80; fatal flaw of, 15; funeral rites
violations by, 5–6, 10, 13, 22–23, 40,
44–45; on Oedipus, 42, 43–44; rule
of, 5–7; violence and, 6–7, 9–11, 13–17
crimes: death and, 27, 28, 33; impossible,
11–12, 17; of Oedipus, 41, 43–44, 50,
52, 66, 68–69; of Polyneices, 53–55,
56; state, as special weapons, 17–18

death, 21–49; Antigone's burial alive, 14–15,
41, 45, 55; coinciding with itself, 25,
39; funeral rites following (*see* funeral
rites); Heidegger's views on, 36–37;
immortality and, 34–35, 37, 45, 46–48,
49, 71; indestructible life and, 27–28, 30,
32–33, 34–35; language relationship
with, 25–26, 37–38, 57; mistreatment
of corpse after, 21–22, 24; regeneration
and, 27–28, 33, 44, 45; resurrection of,
linguistically, 26; second (*see* second
death); sexual reproduction, sexuality,
and, 27, 28–36, 70, 72–73; state vs.
private laws on, 11; torture and,
24, 29–30; traumatic events and, 40;
undeadness and (*see* undeadness);
violence and, 11, 14–15
death drive, 34, 36, 38, 39
"Death of Immortality, The?" (Lefort), 46
decency vs. obscenity, 13–14, 18–20

85

Alenka Zupančič is a Slovenian philosopher and social theorist. She is a professor of philosophy and psychoanalysis at the European Graduate School and a researcher at the Institute of Philosophy at the Slovene Academy of Sciences and Arts. She is the author of many books, including *What Is Sex?* (2017), *The Odd One In: On Comedy* (2008), and *Ethics of the Real: Kant and Lacan* (2000).

INVENTING WRITING THEORY

Jacques Lezra and Paul North, series editors

Werner Hamacher, *Minima Philologica*. Translated by Catharine Diehl and
  Jason Groves
Michal Ben-Naftali, *Chronicle of Separation: On Deconstruction's
  Disillusioned Love*. Translated by Mirjam Hadar. Foreword by Avital Ronell
Daniel Hoffman-Schwartz, Barbara Natalie Nagel, and Lauren Shizuko Stone,
  eds., *Flirtations: Rhetoric and Aesthetics This Side of Seduction*
Jean-Luc Nancy, *Intoxication*. Translated by Philip Armstrong
Márton Dornbach, *Receptive Spirit: German Idealism and the Dynamics of
  Cultural Transmission*
Sean Alexander Gurd, *Dissonance: Auditory Aesthetics in Ancient Greece*
Anthony Curtis Adler, *Celebricities: Media Culture and the Phenomenology of
  Gadget Commodity Life*
Nathan Brown, *The Limits of Fabrication: Materials Science, Materialist
  Poetics*
Jay Bernstein, Adi Ophir, and Ann Laura Stoler, eds., *Political Concepts:
  A Critical Lexicon*
Willy Thayer, *Technologies of Critique*. Translated by John Kraniauskas
Julie Beth Napolin, *The Fact of Resonance: Modernist Acoustics and
  Narrative Form*

Ann Laura Stoler, Stathis Gourgouris, and Jacques Lezra, eds., *Thinking with Balibar: A Lexicon of Conceptual Practice*

Nathan Brown, *Rationalist Empiricism: A Theory of Speculative Critique*

Gerhard Richter, *Thinking with Adorno: The Uncoercive Gaze*

Kevin McLaughlin, *The Philology of Life: Walter Benjamin's Critical Program*

Alenka Zupančič, *Let Them Rot: Antigone's Parallax*

Adi M. Ophir, *In the Beginning Was the State: Divine Violence in the Hebrew Bible*

Printed in the USA
CPSIA information can be obtained
at www.ICGtesting.com
JSHW021327110324
58992JS00007B/326